# CHOOSING A NURSING HOME 2nd Edition

# CHOOSING A NURSING HOME 2nd Edition

**AN INSIDER'S ANALYSIS FULLY UPDATED AND REVISED**

**Dr. Seth B. Goldsmith**

Plus New Sections on Alternatives to Nursing Homes and Medicare Nursing Home Compare Data

ISBN-13: 9781984005533
ISBN-10: 1984005537
Library of Congress Control Number: 2018901451
CreateSpace Independent Publishing Platform
North Charleston, South Carolina

# Dedicated to

*Our senior and disabled citizens, who deserve the best care that we can offer, and to those dedicated families and caregivers who act in the best interests of our seniors and disabled men, women, and children.*

# Acknowledgments

For me, writing a second edition of a previously published book had its own special challenges, including what to retain and what to discard as well as how to deal with the myriad changes that have occurred in the past three decades. Many long-term-care professionals have generously helped me in this new endeavor. To the following people, I am particularly grateful: Tim Lukenda, Dylan Mann, Alvan Small, Don Shulman, Leonard Thaler, Frank DaSilva, Jeff Cohen, Dr. Joshua Gortler, Rabbi Samuel Sandhaus, Steve Willens, Fred Stock, Beth Kofsky, Charlie Schewe, Lowell and Carol Goldsmith, and Governor Howard Dean.

Special thanks to the *Kaiser Health News* for permitting me to republish Jordan Rau's article of December 31, 2017, titled, "Care Suffers as More Nursing Homes Feed Money into Corporate Webs." Thanks also to Patricia L. McGinnis, executive director of the California Advocates for Nursing Homes Reform for granting me permission to republish their document "Fact Sheet on Nursing Home Agreements" (Appendix 4). Additionally, thanks to a certain dear friend and nursing-home administrator who has shared with me a great deal of his experiences and insights as well as the nursing-home admission agreement found in Appendix 3.

Finally, thanks to my wife, Wendy Benjamin, who provided me with enormous support throughout this project.

# Contents

Preface · · · · · · · · · · · · · · · · · · · · · · · · · · · · · · · · · · · · · · · · xix

Chapter 1 Introduction · · · · · · · · · · · · · · · · · · · · · · · · · · · · · · · · · · · · · 1

The Importance of Timing in Decision Making · · · · · · · · · · · · · 5

Chapter 2 Understanding the Basics of Nursing Homes · · · · · · · · · · · · · · · 8

A Few Numbers · · · · · · · · · · · · · · · · · · · · · · · · · · · · · · · · · · · · · 8

Nursing Homes: Custodial Facilities or Rehabiliation Units? · · · 9

Nursing Homes and Nursing Facilities: What Exactly are they? · · · · · · · · · · · · · · · · · · · · · · · · · · · · · · · · · · · · · · · · · 10

Chapter 3 Understanding the Basics of Assisted Living · · · · · · · · · · · · · · · 12

Chapter 4 Understanding the Basics of NORCs, Independent-Living Facilities, CCRCs, and Home Health Care · · · · · · · · · · · · · · · · · · 14

NORCs (Naturally Occurring Retirement Communities) · · · · 14

Independent-Living Facilities · · · · · · · · · · · · · · · · · · · · · · · · · · · · · · 15

CCRCs (Continuing-Care Retirement Communities) · · · · · · · · 17

Home Health Care · · · · · · · · · · · · · · · · · · · · · · · · · · · · · · · · · · · · · · · · 20

A Final Word about Aging in Place · · · · · · · · · · · · · · · · · · · · · · · · 23

Chapter 5 The Basics of Paying for Nursing-Home Care · · · · · · · · · · · · · · · 24

Introduction · · · · · · · · · · · · · · · · · · · · · · · · · · · · · · · · · · · · · · · · · · · · · 24

Medicare (And a Bit of History) · · · · · · · · · · · · · · · · · · · · · · · · · · · 24

Medicaid · · · · · · · · · · · · · · · · · · · · · · · · · · · · · · · · · · · · · · · · · · · · · · · · 27

Long-Term-Care Insurance · · · · · · · · · · · · · · · · · · · · · · · · · · · · · · · · 29

Sorting through the Confusion · · · · · · · · · · · · · · · · · · · · · · · · · · · · 30

Key Questions (And Answers) · · · · · · · · · · · · · · · · · · · · · · · · · · · · · 31

Chapter 6 Organizational Issues · · · · · · · · · · · · · · · · · · · · · · · · · · · · · · · · · · 39

Nursing-Home Ownership: Implications · · · · · · · · · · · · · · · · · · · 39

Management Issues · · · 51
Medical-Staff Issues · · · 55
Nursing-Staff Issues · · · 57
Social-Services Issues · · · 59
Physical Therapy, Occupational Therapy and
Speech-Language Pathology Therapy Services · · · 60
Activities and Recreational Services · · · 62
Staffing the Remainder of the Organization · · · 64
Hospital and Nursing-Home Relationships · · · 65
Chapter 7 The Need for a Nursing Home · · · 67
Introduction · · · 67
The Residents' Perspective · · · 68
The Family's Perspective · · · 70
The Physician's Perspective · · · 76
The Bureaucratic Perspective · · · 78
Conclusion · · · 81

Chapter 8 The Costs of Nursing Homes and Alternative Long-Term-Care Options · · · · · 83
Nursing Homes · · · · · 83
Assisted-Living Communities · · · · · 85
The Staying-Home Alternative · · · · · 87
Adult Day Care · · · · · 88
The Pace Programs (Program of All-Inclusive Care for the Elderly) · · · · · 89
Design Options for Staying at Home · · · · · 90
Medicare and Medicaid Payments · · · · · 92
Charges, Cost, and Quality · · · · · 92
Chapter 9 Quality—The Elusive Component · · · · · 94
Introduction · · · · · 94
Defining Quality · · · · · 95
Distinguishing Quality of Care from Quality of Life · · · · · 97
The Bad News about Quality · · · · · 99

Indicators and Pseudo-Indicators of Quality ···· 102

Indicator 1: Licensure of the Nursing Home ···· 102

Indicator 2: Gold Stars, Gold Seals, and Medals ···· 103

Indicator 3: Licensure of Administrator ···· 104

Indicator 4: Medicare and Medicaid Certification ···· 105

Indicator 5: Organizational Memberships ···· 105

Indicator 6: Accreditation Status ···· 106

Indicator 7: Teaching Affiliations ···· 107

Some Final Issues on Quality ···· 108

Chain Homes, Hospital-Owned Facilities, Nonprofit Facilities, and Mom and Pop Homes ···· 108

Special-Focus Facilities and Facilities under Corporate Integrity Agreements (CIAs) ···· 109

Conclusion ···· 110

Chapter 10 Being an Educated Consumer—Finding the Right Home ···· 111

Selecting a Location ···· 113

Using the Internet to Search and Research Nursing Homes ........ 115
What You Can Learn from www.medicare.gov ........ 116
The US Government's Nursing Home Compare Site ........ 116
Using the Medicare Nursing-Home-Compare Website: An Illustration ........ 125
Four Caveats about the Medicare.gov Data ........ 130
Still Photos and Old Data ........ 130
Significant Issues with the Five-Star System ........ 131
The Best Survey Is Your Own Multiple Field Trips—*Trips, Not Trip!* ........ 131
Location-Location-Location ........ 132
Chapter 11 The Preliminary Nursing-Home Visit ........ 133
Purposes of the Preliminary Visit ........ 133
The Preliminary-Visit Team ........ 134

Arranging the Visit · · · 134
The Interviewees and Areas of Inquiry · · · 136
Interviewing the Administrator · · · 137
Interviewing the Nursing Director · · · 141
Interviewing the Social-Services Director · · · 143
Interviewing the Activities Director · · · 145
Meeting with Residents · · · 146
Observations During the Visit · · · 148
The Smell Test · · · 148
Cleanliness · · · 148
Observe the Residents · · · 149
Observe the Staff · · · 149
Analyzing the Information · · · 150
Threshold Question · · · 150
Tearing and Comparing · · · 150

Chapter 12 The Crucial Second Look ........ 151
Being Prepared: Two Steps ........ 151
Google and Bing the Home, Its Owners, and Its Parent Company ........ 151
Do a Second Review of the Home's Most Recent Medicare Survey ........ 152
Obtaining Recommendations ........ 152
Recommendations from Care Providers ........ 154
Using the Data from the References ........ 157
The Second Visit and New Questions ........ 158
Areas for Additional Observation ........ 162
Decisions and Deals ........ 163
Chapter 13 Finding a First-Class Nursing Home: The Elements of Excellence ........ 165
Introduction ........ 165
Element 1: Mission ........ 166
Element 2: Economic Orientation ........ 166

Element 3: Governance · · · 167

Element 4: Medical Staff · · · 168

Element 5: Nursing · · · 168

Element 6: Therapeutic Services · · · 169

Element 7: Activities · · · 170

Element 8: Physical Facilities · · · 170

Element 9: Top-Level Managerial Sensitivity · · · 171

A Final Word · · · 172

Appendices

Appendix 1 Nursing-Home Checklist · · · 175

Appendix 2 Residents' Rights and Protections · · · 183

Appendix 3 Example of a Long-Term-Care Contract · · · 191

Appendix 4 Fact Sheet on Nursing-Home Agreements Reprinted With Permission from California Advocates for Nursing Home Reform · · · 219

# Preface

Hurricane Irma began its march into Florida on Friday morning, September 10, 2017, making landfall at Cudjoe Key, a 5.2-square-mile island located 110 miles southwest of Miami and 20 miles east of Key West. After unleashing its destructive force on that small island, it moved up the Keys and visited the rest of the state with powerful winds, rains, and flooding.

Among the saddest of all stories resulting from Irma occurred in my home community of Hollywood, Florida. The internationally reported tragedy began in the early hours of September 13 when the Rehabilitation Center of Hollywood Hills (RCHH) put in its first 911 call about the deaths of several elderly nursing-home residents. Within weeks, the number of deaths connected with RCHH totaled fourteen! On November 22, 2017, the Hollywood Police Department issued a media release that stated that the Broward County medical examiner had determined that twelve of the fourteen deaths at the nursing home should be ruled as "homicide with the cause of death attributed to environmental heat exposures."

As I write this preface, a few months after the initial incident, I am mindful of the fact that there are presently multiple lawsuits filed in both federal and local courts as well as a great deal of finger pointing. The owners of this 152-bed for-profit nursing home are claiming that Florida Power and Light (FPL) dropped the ball because it failed to heed the home's calls for help.

The owners are also pointing a finger at Florida's governor Rick Scott, who they claim did not respond to telephone messages and calls made to the governor's private cell-phone line from the nursing home's management. Families of the fourteen residents whose deaths may be tied to the care their loved ones received, or did not receive, during the storm hurricane or shortly thereafter, are busy filing lawsuits claiming negligence and likely elder abuse. As of January 2018, the City of Hollywood Police Department is continuing its investigation into those twelve deaths that have been ruled as homicides.

In the state capitol of Tallahassee, politicians have responded to this horrible situation by introducing more than a dozen pieces of legislation that would require both nursing homes and assisted-living facilities to have emergency generators as well as at least ninety-six hours of fuel to power the generators. Additional oversight and monitoring with cameras are also proposed. How this legislation will fare is an open question. A generator to power a typical nursing home could cost hundreds of thousands of dollars to install and many thousands a year to maintain. I do not anticipate much support on this bill from the long-term-care industry!

A few weeks after the hurricane, I drove past the almost block-long rehabilitation facility/nursing home. It is a two-story building initially constructed in 1968 with modifications in 1972 and 1989. Stationed in front of the totally evacuated building was a Hollywood police officer sitting in a marked black-and-white Ford Crown Victoria. Surrounding the entirety of the structure is yellow plastic crime-scene tape. As of February 2018, the building remains shuttered.

Regardless of the accusations, lawsuits,, newspaper or magazine articles, and TV reports, here is the most important piece of information: fourteen fragile people ranging in age from fifty-seven to ninety-nine died either in that nursing home or their death can be linked to the failure to evacuate them from the unhealthy tropical heat of that building. The seriousness of the situation at RCHH was emphasized on January 31, 2018, by the court testimony of a Broward County EMT who responded to a call from the nursing home and found patients whose body temperature exceeded 107 degrees. But for the behavior of the management and staff that day, fourteen human beings might still be alive. Additionally, had these people been in a different facility, their families and friends would not be mourning their loss.

So for any family the overarching question remains: How do you select a nursing facility for a loved one? Do you just go to the closest place or the home with the most elegant lobby? Or is your choice limited to where your doctor or the hospital's discharge planner tells you to go? As is obvious from the next chapter, I am a pro in this long-term-care industry, and this book is designed for consumers who wish to be proactive about a move that could be a life or death decision for a loved family member or friend.

# CHAPTER 1

# Introduction

In 1990 I wrote a book titled *Choosing a Nursing Home* (published by Prentice-Hall Press) that was focused on helping consumers make life and family-altering decisions about long-term care. The book was successful simply because it found its way into the hands of many consumers and onto the bookshelves of numerous libraries—perhaps as a result of it being selected a "Book of the Year" by the *Library Journal*. More importantly for me, it was also a personally gratifying book because I was fortunate enough to hear from scores of families, social workers, and nursing-home residents who shared their experiences of using the book as part of their own process of making a decision to select a nursing home for a loved one.

At the time I wrote the *Choosing* book, my own experiences were primarily those of a university-based professor. In addition to my teaching and research on long-term care, I had served on nonprofit boards and consulted with a broad range of health-care organizations. Additionally, I augmented those experiences with a Robert Wood Johnson Foundation–funded summer fellowship at the Jewish Nursing Home of western Massachusetts. Once the decision was made to write the *Choosing* book, I logged more than twenty-five thousand miles of travel visiting fifty nursing homes in twenty-two states and interviewing hundreds of their staff and residents.

The result was a book that was different from the others of its genre by its numerous examples of nursing homes throughout the country that offered interesting and valuable programs for residents. By writing about these state-of-the-art and innovative places, I was able to demonstrate that a good nursing home placement decision could very well lead to an enriched and meaningful life for a loved one even after institutionalization. In essence I was able to offer evidence that given the right situation, placement in a nursing home was the beginning of a valuable chapter in one's life.

In the years subsequent to the publishing of the book, I have become a true "nursing home junkie." In fact I continued my personal touring, and as of 2017 I've visited at least a hundred more nursing homes and assisted-living centers in the United States as well as facilities in various Canadian provinces, France, England, Wales, Holland, and Israel.

From a productivity standpoint, I have written articles on nursing homes, been quoted in the *New York Times*, appeared on numerous television and radio programs about nursing homes, written and edited two academic textbooks on long-term care administration, written a monograph for boards of directors, sponsored by the Commonwealth Fund, consulted at many nursing homes, represented nursing homes as an attorney, served on trade association boards, been given awards for my work in long-term care, taught graduate courses on long-term-care administration, and had the following extremely significant personal and professional experiences.

On a personal level, a great deal has changed in my life since I wrote *Choosing a Nursing Home*. The most obvious change to occur is that I have become a senior citizen! Yet based on current statistics, I am still at least one decade away from being an "average" nursing-home resident. Additionally, I have gone through what many of us in the sandwich generation have experienced, that is, I had an elderly widowed mother who at the age of eighty-nine needed to be moved out of her condominium and into an independent-living residence that also functioned as an assisted-living facility.

Five years later my brother, a retired medical-school professor and dean, and I had to arrange intensive and extensive home care in order to allow our mother to stay in her new residence until she died at the age of ninety-four. Her death was quiet, peaceful, and dignified. She died in the bed that my dad and she had bought more than fifty years earlier and that had journeyed with her from our house in Brooklyn, to her condo in North Miami Beach, and finally, to her independent-living facility in Miami. The last year of her life journey cost in excess of $120,000 for round-the-clock aides, a price that she reluctantly paid but could afford for a good end-of-life period.

Unfortunately for our family, while Mom was aging in Florida, another problematic situation was unfolding in the Springfield suburb of Longmeadow, Massachusetts, at the Jewish Nursing Home (JNH), a not-for-profit organization that I had been on the board since the late 1980s. In 1993, my younger sister, who had lived in Lakeland, Florida, for thirteen years and was a victim of multiple sclerosis (and later cancer), was admitted to the JNH. For the next twelve years, she lived at the nursing home and touched so many people that moments after her passing, the CEO called my brother and me and requested that we delay her burial in New York so that the following morning the nursing home could hold an in-house funeral service for our sister. The experience, as a family member, of the incredible kindness shown by the JNH staff over more than a decade, as well as the hundreds of people who attended that early morning service, was both moving and enormously instructive. The lessons I learned at the JNH, as well as from my sister who proved to be a keen observer of resident life, taught me a great deal that I hope to share in this book.

On the professional side, three important things happened to me subsequent to the writing of *Choosing a Nursing Home*. First, I was able to expand my law and consulting practices to actively encompass long-term-care organizations and issues. Among my clients whose projects were instrumental in my continuing growth were trade associations and nursing homes. Second, in 1995, I was elected to the board of directors of Extendicare, a Toronto-based publicly traded company (primarily on the Toronto Stock Exchange) that at one time owned and operated close to five hundred nursing homes, assisted-living facilities, home-care providers, and other related businesses in the United States and Canada. In January 2016, I retired from the board after twenty-one years of service and was awarded the title of director emeritus. During my years with Extendicare, I served not only as a member of the board but also as the chair of the quality/standards committee and a member of the audit committee. During those years I had a front-row seat and observed and participated in decisions made by one of the largest for-profit companies in the long-term-care industry. Several years ago Extendicare decided to sell all its holdings in the United States and concentrate on owning, operating, and managing nursing homes, assisted-living facilities, and home-care programs in Canada. This was a decision I fully supported.

The third new major experience that informs the writing of this new consumer-oriented book is that in 1996 the Miami Jewish Home and Hospital for the Aged, the largest geriatric system in the southern United States, hired me to be chief executive officer of their organization. For more than two years, I was CEO of this not-for-profit business that owned many corporations, including a five-hundred-bed nursing home, a thirty-two-bed geriatric hospital, three adult day-care centers, a busy medical clinic, a rehabilitation center, a geriatric research institute, an independent-living facility (where my mother lived), an assisted-living facility (that was being built and is now fully occupied), and numerous other programs and facilities. During those years I spent countless hours speaking with thousands of staff, residents, their families, and others involved in the world of long-term care.

When I wrote *Choosing a Nursing Home*, almost three decades ago, I noted that the starting point for my research had been a visit in the early 1960s to a nursing home in Brooklyn, New York, where my eighty-year-old maternal grandfather spent the last months of his life in a hot, crowded ward that stank with the smell of urine. Now, more than a half century later, I am still repulsed by that place and uncertain how and why my family moved him into that dreadful facility. My grandfather's story was not dissimilar to those of many others of his generation. From the time of his becoming a widower in 1941, he lived primarily with his daughter (my aunt Evelyn) and her family. Occasionally my aunt Evelyn would get a break, and my grandfather would come visit my family for a few weeks or perhaps stay at the home of another aunt. However, it was quite clear to all of us that Grandpa primarily lived with Evelyn in a small bedroom with a stack of Yiddish newspapers, his collection of pipes, and the familiar pungent odor of Prince Albert tobacco.

Unfortunately I never asked any of my relatives about my grandfather's living arrangements and regrettably they are all now dead. Despite my lack of formal evidence, my conclusion is that his placement in the nursing home was a painful decision for my aunt and the family. Like most people I've met in the same or similar situations, his placement was probably a last resort, happening when his failing health placed too great care burden on the family and there were no financial resources to hire outside help.

My grandfather's situation essentially fits within a model I often talk about in my lectures. Simply stated, the model suggests that there are three ways to avoid nursing homes. First (and clearly not desirable), die young. For the most part, nursing homes are filled with the elderly—very few people who are middle aged are residents unless they are there for short-term rehabilitation or a disabling chronic disease. The second way to avoid a nursing home is to have great wealth. If a person has enough money, he or she can essentially have a round-the-clock private staff caring for him or her. But we are talking about hundreds of thousands of dollars for extended periods of times, perhaps years—the average nursing-home stay being in the two-and-a-half-year range. The third option, and the one my grandfather almost had, is to have lots of daughters. I do not want to sound sexist, but the data supports the idea that if there are enough daughters (around five), then the probability of winding up in a nursing home decreases significantly. My grandfather had four, but he still wound up in a nursing home for the last few months of his life. Without the daughters he probably would have been in a home much sooner.

## The Importance of Timing in Decision Making

For anyone considering a move into a nursing home, time is your best friend and worst enemy. As a friend, it gives you the opportunity to search out all the alternatives discussed in other sections of this book. Some of these alternatives such as developing a homegrown and administered nursing home at home take time to implement. For example, it is imperative that the right people are hired to deliver the care and that the hardware of care, such as the proper bed or suction equipment, is in place.

Time may also be required to get a loved one to the top of a waiting list. My advice to everyone is the same—if you are the least bit interested, put your name on the list even if an application fee is required. It is much better to have the option when you need it than not have the option. In some states admission to a nursing home is on a fairly strict "first come, first served" basis regardless of payment source. In those instances, as well as when a nursing home has the reputation for being the best in a community or the best for a specific population, waiting lists can be long. However, even long lists do clear because there is a turnover of beds in nursing homes and people drop off the lists for reasons ranging from death to alternative arrangements. Getting your name on the list is equally important for assisted-living facilities and CCRCs! More about this issue later.

Time will also allow a family to work out any financial arrangements necessary to pay for the care. These arrangements may involve anything from applying for medical assistance to finding the resources to pay for private care. Along similar lines, time will allow the family and the resident to prepare for the difficult and often heart-wrenching transition into the nursing home.

Time, or more specifically lack of time, can also be an enemy. For example, this lack of time tends to generate enormous stress when a hospital pressures a family to move a loved one out of an expensive hospital bed into a lower cost nursing-home bed.

To the extent possible, families should buy as much time as possible by advance planning, that is, studying up on nursing homes by reading this book and visiting potential homes where a loved one might be placed. Time can also be bought by not taking what is proffered on face value. Indeed, do not let the hospital's pressure to make a placement get in the way of a family's better judgment about what is in the best interests of a loved one.

It is crucial to realize that every move that is made is very draining on the sick or elderly person being moved. In the professional literature, this is called "transfer trauma," and the term is a precise statement of the problem. To the extent feasible moves should be kept to a minimum. For example, I know of numerous instances when an elderly person was moved to one facility only to be moved to another a few weeks later. If possible, avoid the two-step dance—it's harmful to one's health.

In the next chapter, I will review the basics of nursing homes so that we are all operating with the language and general understanding of nursing homes—what they are and how they function.

# CHAPTER 2

# Understanding the Basics of Nursing Homes

*Nobody thinks that going into a nursing home is going to happening to him or her…nobody prepares himself or herself for this. They think they are going to live forever the way they are living.*

—Mr. S.F., eighty-year-old nursing-home resident, Louisville, Kentucky

## A Few Numbers

Over 1.3 million persons reside in America's 15,640 certified nursing homes with an operational capacity of approximately 1.7 million beds. Taking care of the needs of these people, twenty-four hours a day and seven days a week, are approximately 1.6 million staff, most of whom are nurse's aides. On average each nursing-home resident receives 4.1 hours of nursing care per day; however, most of that care is not provided by registered nurses (RNs) or licensed practical nurses (LPNs) but rather by nonlicensed and minimally trained nurses' aides or nursing assistants. Over half of the residents are more than eighty-five years old, and more than 70 percent are women, most often white.

As with many health statistics, there are wide variations throughout the country. While the nationwide occupancy rate is approximately 82 percent, on a state-by-state basis, we see significant differences. In the District of Columbia, occupancy is at 93 percent, both North and South Dakota at 92 percent, Rhode Island at 91 percent, and New York at 90 percent. At the low end of the occupancy chart are Utah at 64 percent, Oregon at 65 percent, and Oklahoma and Montana at 66 percent. From a practical standpoint, these numbers mean that in certain states and communities, the consumer will likely have more options and perhaps time to make a decision than in other places.

In the high-occupancy states, while getting on a waiting list for the most desired home is a good strategy, the crisis that may precipitate a placement may also not coincide with bed availability. In those cases it may be necessary to move someone into a less attractive nursing home and wait until a bed is available at the desired home and then organize a transfer. One nursing-home CEO suggested to me another approach for high-occupancy areas. This method might work when a family foresees the likelihood of a loved one needing custodial care subsequent to a period of rehabilitation. His idea is simply to make sure that the rehabilitation placement is in the same facility where the family wants to place the loved one for custodial care. During the rehabilitation period at the skilled-nursing facility (SNF), he suggests working with the SNF's discharge planner to transfer the resident into the custodial care part of the facility at the end of the rehab period. This administrator noted, "As long as the [loved one's] needs can be met at the SNF, and a payer source is eventually out there, the SNF is obligated to keep [the resident]."

## Nursing Homes: Custodial Facilities or Rehabiliation Units?

Further confounding this discussion about nursing homes is that many facilities function in dual roles not only as a permanent home for the frail elderly but also as rehabilitation center for patients recovering from injuries or illness such as strokes, heart attacks, or surgery. For example, a few years ago, I toured the new rehabilitation floor of a facility in the Boston area. Prior to an extensive renovation on the second floor of the nursing-home building, rehabilitation patients were often found throughout the other floors of the nursing home, that is, wherever a bed was available. The rehabilitation short timers ate their meals in the same dining room with the long-term residents and shared the rehabilitation room space with these residents.

In the judgment of the administrator, as well as the parent company that owned the nursing home, this arrangement was detrimental to the success of the rehabilitation program. It was their opinion that rehabilitation patients were not interested in interacting with residents and that from a marketing perspective, a separate and distinct unit would make the rehab program more competitive. Thus, an entire floor was designated as the rehabilitation unit. It was totally renovated from top to bottom and a private dining room as well as private rehabilitation space was developed on the floor. Thereafter, the unit operated in separate quarters from the nursing home providing residents with a clear sense of being in a short-term rehabilitation facility and not a nursing home.

The next sections of this chapter will be devoted to understanding the "language" of nursing homes and related facilities as well as the most critical, financial, staff, and programmatic aspects of these facilities. In this next section, I shall begin with "official" definitions and then clarify these distinctions in less jargon-laden terms.

## Nursing Homes and Nursing Facilities: What Exactly are they?

While the same physical facility may serve as both a nursing home and a nursing facility, the federal government's primary agency responsible for Medicare and Medicaid, the Centers for Medicare & Medicaid Services (CMS), defines these organizations as follows:

***Nursing Facility***: *A facility which primarily provides to residents skilled nursing care and related services for the rehabilitation of injured, disabled, or sick persons, or on a regular basis, health related care services above the level of custodial care to other than mentally retarded individuals.*

***Nursing Home***: *A residence that provides a room, meals, and help with the activities of daily living and recreation. Generally, nursing home residents have* *physical or mental problems that keep them from living on their own. They usually require daily assistance.*

These two definitions illustrate some of the essential and technical differences between the plain vanilla nursing home and the skilled-nursing facility (SNF). In the past these two types of organizations were called SNFs and ICFs (intermediate care facilities). For reasons that are unclear, these distinctions were eliminated about two decades ago. So now we have what are essentially rehabilitation facilities and programs designed to be short-term with the goal of returning the resident to his or her home back in the community. In order to accomplish this goal, the facility is staffed with a broad range of therapists such as speech therapists, occupational therapists, and physical therapists.

On the other hand, the nursing home is for "custody" of the resident and the focus is long-term care, meaning support for the activities of daily living and perhaps some stimulation through recreational and activity programs. Sometimes some of these programs may appear to have a therapeutic value, but more often they are designed to "hold the line." Rarely is it anticipated that someone will be able to make the transition back to community living from custodian living in a nursing home. Further, few nursing homes even offer programs or resources to assist the residents in making such a transition. The nursing home then is generally a person's last residential stop in life.

# CHAPTER 3

## Understanding the Basics of Assisted Living

The CMS defines assisted living as "a type of living arrangement in which personal care services such as meals, housekeeping, transportation, and assistance with activities of daily living are available as needed to people who still live on their own in a residential facility. In most cases, the 'assisted living' residents pay a regular monthly rent. Then, they typically pay additional fees for the services they get."

As assisted-living facilities have proliferated, they have come under increased regulations from the state. However, there are distinct differences in nomenclature from state to state, so in Washington assisted-living facilities are licensed under "boarding house" regulations; in New York a distinction is made between adult homes, assisted-living residences, and enriched assisted-living residences. For example, the laws of Massachusetts ,651 CMR section 12: Department of Elder Affairs, are thirty-one pages long and regulates virtually everything that occurs in an assisted living facility including bathing, dressing, ambulation, meals, housekeeping, self administered medication management, emergency care, financial management of resident funds, recreational activities as well as record keeping, staff training and resident rights.

In reality, assisted-living facilities come in all sizes and shapes. Some are small and rather basic, while others, such as the one I was privileged to be involved with during my tenure at the Miami Jewish Home, the Hazel Cypen Tower in Miami, Florida. This ninety-two-unit building housed a synagogue (also used by the nursing-home and independent-living residents of the Miami Jewish Home), a therapeutic swimming pool, and a gym. Typically many of the facilities that I have visited also have some type of twenty-four-hour self-service juice/snack bar with cereals and cookies, a library, and a common room for activities. The goal of assisted living is typically to provide a safe and stimulating environment that is more homelike and less institutional.

Others might be small, privately owned facilities, often converted homes in residential neighborhoods with only six beds. Such facilities require licensure in most states and must also meet a range of health and safety requirements. For example, in Florida post the tragedy at the Rehabilitation Center of Hollywood Hills in September 2017, the State Department of Elder Affairs issued a new rule that required assisted-living facilities to have a plan and to implement that plan so that if there is a loss of electrical power, the temperature in the facility can be maintained at eighty degrees Fahrenheit for a minimum of ninety-six hours. Or to put it differently, the state basically wants to require all facilities to have a generator that works! In fact in Florida, we now have over a dozen new legislative bills designed to safeguard the institutionalized elderly.

The danger for all consumers though is the small, unlicensed facility. Effectively using such a facility is putting the future of the elderly or infirm in the hands of a caregiver with no oversight. In my opinion it is asking for trouble.

# CHAPTER 4

# Understanding the Basics of NORCs, Independent-Living Facilities, CCRCs, and Home Health Care

## NORCs (Naturally Occurring Retirement Communities)

In the summer of 1951, my family along with my uncle, aunt, and two cousins drove from New York to Miami. Along the way we stopped in St. Petersburg, Florida, to visit what was billed as Doc Webb's Drug Store, the "most unusual drug store in the world." Sitting outside the store, my forty-six-year-old uncle confided in me that someday he was going to retire to Florida. That day came in 1967 and little did he, and later my mother, know that they were in the forefront of what today is known as the NORCs. Basically these are exactly what they sound like, places where people move when they are relatively healthy new retirees and where they stay when they get older and frail and need services. What makes any of this possible is services, either health services or social services.

The formally identified NORCs (eligible for federal monies) typically provide some services to residents, including social services, recreational activities, and some preventive health services. In the most sophisticated programs, a host of additional services can be provided that make the NORC look like an assisted-living program with independent housing for its participants.

At the minimalist end of the NORC spectrum is the independent living that comes as two types. One type is simply totally independent, a house, room, or apartment. No services, no support, no food, nothing! This is the way my mother lived in Florida for almost thirty years. She had a one-bedroom condominium in a building whose only recreational facilities were a card room, pool table, and swimming pool. For most of those thirty years, that is all she needed. She stayed busy with her friends and relatives, traveling working as treasurer of the condominium, shopping, and playing a nightly canasta game. At the other end of the spectrum is the more organized and typically institutionally based independent-living facility.

## Independent-Living Facilities

Continuing with the story about my mother, as well as thousands of other elderly relatives, as Mom approached her eighty-seventh birthday, she began feeling isolated. Her social circle, largely composed of fellow residents from her condo, had shrunk through death or moves to a nursing home. Additionally, her general stamina appeared to be slowing down, perhaps because of inadequate nutrition or lack of stimulation. After many family meetings, as well as an outstanding geriatric assessment, she reluctantly agreed to move (on a trial basis) into an independent-living facility, the Irving Cypen Tower (ICT) at the Miami Jewish Home, as long as we did not sell her condo. The deal was simple. She paid $1,900 per month for a small one-bedroom apartment that included a full-size bathroom and decent eat-in kitchen. The monthly fee included a full-course sit-down dinner every night (with enough leftovers for a meal the following day); numerous social activities every day and almost every evening; transportation for food shopping, the bank, or mall shopping; weekly housekeeping; and a secure environment. Within a month, her mood was elevated, and she was eating quite well and began enjoying life with a host of new friends. She told my brother and me to sell the condo—she was staying at ICT.

The seven years that she lived there were truly a blessing. She became an active volunteer at the nursing home, attended countless concerts and theater performances, and truly enjoyed the last years of her life with staff who were kind and attentive. Incidentally, for the last five of her seven years at the Miami Jewish Home, I was no longer employed at the Home. The programs she participated in with her new friends insured that she was rarely isolated and always felt physically secure. Even in the last few months of her life when she had developed esophageal cancer, the staff worked with us so that she never had to move into the nursing-home part of the facility. Aides stayed with her (at an extra expense), and the dining services always accommodated her with the proper foods properly prepared (as part of their services). This is an example of the best of services.

For some elderly a move from a longtime residence can be avoided with modifications to make their home more senior user friendly. For example, in a bathroom grab bars for the tub or the toilet can be installed. Perhaps a raised toilet seat could make life easier for some people. Other modifications such as enhanced lighting, lowered kitchen cabinets, or ramps may also make it possible to stay at home. Particularly valuable are emergency-alert systems that have the capability of bringing emergency-response terms to the caller within minutes. Chapter 8 provides additional information about this *staying at home* option.

Health-care facilities that are committed to the concept of "aging in place" can often make a difference in the life of the elderly. For example, in my consulting practice, I was once privileged to work with a nonprofit board in Southern California that operated an attractive new retirement community for active seniors. In fact the first group of two hundred people who moved into the facility were retired executives, professionals, and business people with expensive cars parked behind the facility. For the most part, they were people who had been tired of maintaining large homes with unneeded space and preferred the simplicity of an upscale community. They regularly dined out, went to sporting and entertainment venues, and traveled outside the area and indeed, the country.

But over time many of this first group of residents suffered the diseases of aging and were left as less active people often with wheelchairs and walkers and needing assistance. The board and management decided to accommodate them with a host of services, and on my last visit, approximately 25 percent of the residents were essentially in *assisted living* with the other 75 percent in independent living. Despite this statistical situation, no one was moved to a more intense level of care such as a skilled-nursing facility.

Instead the residents were treated as if they were in their own homes and services, essentially wrapped around those who required nursing care or other therapies. This then is another example of *aging in place*. Finally it should be noted that in the management of this facility, newcomers are only eligible for admission as independent-living residents, and there must be a clear expectation that they will be that way many months into the future. This too is a reasonable accommodation in a mixed-use facility.

## CCRCs (Continuing-Care Retirement Communities)

The concept behind the more than eighteen hundred CCRCs in the United States is truly outstanding and quite close to the concept of "aging in place." The reality can be perfectly on target or very disappointing. It is also an expensive option! The advice one should heed about CCRCs is that one should approach moving into a CCRC with the kind of thought and deliberation that is usually reserved for any major purchase such as a house or car. Observe, test-drive, ask others, observe again, test-drive, and when the contract is presented to you, read it carefully and have your family lawyer and accountant review the document.

The essence of a CCRC is that it is a senior age-restricted community with multiple levels of housing and care, that is, independent housing, assisted living, and skilled-nursing-home care. In a common model of CCRCs, each level of care is on the same campus usually in connected buildings. Other times the CCRCs, also known as life-care communities, have contracts with other organizations guaranteeing them beds, such as nursing-home space for their members.

In 2010, the US Government Accountability Office (GAO) issued a report titled *Continuing Care Retirement Communities Can Provide Benefits, but Not without Some Risk.* (GAO-10-611). The following are some pertinent excerpts from that report:

*CCRCs are generally residential facilities established in a campus-like setting that provide access for older Americans to three levels of housing and care: independent homes or apartments where residents live much as they did in their own homes; assisted living, which provides help with the daily tasks of living; and skilled nursing care for those with greater physical needs. Most residents must be able to live independently when they enter into a contract with a CCRC, with the intent of moving through the three levels of care as their needs change.* (GAO report, 3)

*CCRCs are primarily regulated by states rather than by the federal government. State CCRC regulation developed over time and in some instances grew out of the need to address financial and consumer protection issues, including insolvency, which arose in the CCRC industry in the 1970s and 1980s. States generally license CCRC providers, monitor and oversee their financial condition, and have regulatory provisions designed to inform and protect consumers. The U.S. Department of Health and Human Services (HHS) provides oversight of nursing facilities that are commonly part of CCRCs, but this oversight focuses on the quality of care and safety of residents in those facilities that receive payments under the Medicare and Medicaid programs.* (GAO report, 3–4)

*CCRCs typically offer one of three general types of contracts that involve different combinations of entrance and monthly fee payments. Some CCRCs may offer residents a choice of the following contract types, while others may choose to offer only one.*

- *Type A, extensive or Life Care contracts, include housing, residential services, and amenities—including unlimited use of health care services—at little or no increase in monthly fees as a resident moves from independent living to assisted living, and, if needed, to nursing care. Type A contracts generally feature substantial entrance fees but may be attractive because monthly payments do not increase substantially as residents move through the different levels of care. As a result, CCRCs absorb the risk of any increases in the cost of providing health and long-term care to residents with these contracts.*
- *Type B, or modified contracts, often have lower monthly fees than Type A contracts, and include the same housing and residential amenities as Type A contracts. However, only some health care services*

*are included in the initial monthly fee. When a resident's needs exceed those services, the fees increase to market rates. For example, a resident may receive 30, 60, or 90 days of assisted living or nursing care without an increased charge. Thereafter, residents would pay the market daily rate or a discounted daily rate—as determined by the CCRC—for all assisted living or nursing care required and face the risk of having to pay high costs for needed care.*

- *Type C, or fee-for-service contracts, include the same housing, residential services, and amenities as Type A and B arrangements but require residents to pay market rates for all health-related services on an as-needed basis. Type C contracts may involve lower entrance and monthly fees while a resident resides in independent living, but the risk of higher long-term care expenses rests with the resident.*
- *Some CCRCs offer a fourth type of contract, Type D or rental agreements, which generally require no entrance fee but guarantee access to CCRC services and health care. Type D contracts are essentially pay-as-you-go:*
- *CCRCs charge monthly fees of residents based on the size of the living unit and the services and care provided.*
- *According to CCRC providers, prospective residents are generally screened to determine their general health status in order to determine the best living situation. Prospective residents must also submit detailed financial information that includes income and tax records to ensure that they can pay CCRC fees over time. Industry participants noted that entry fees—typically made as a large lump-sum payment—can represent a...substantial portion if not all of a potential residents' assets.* (GAO report, 5–6)

For example, recently I discussed the CCRC economic options with a close relative who was considering moving into a well-established facility that is organized as a not-for-profit corporation. According to the website of that particular CCRC, 400 people were living on the campus and were cared for by a workforce of 275 employees. At the independent-living level, this place offers a choice of three different-sized twenty-two-hundred-plus-square-foot single-family homes complete with two-car garages! The next size down are their cottages that start at twelve hundred square feet and go up to sixteen hundred plus square feet—this time with covered parking. The third living options are one- and two-bedroom apartments all with balconies or patios. The facility also has its own nursing home, assisted-living center, and therapy center. It is an amenity-filled CCRC with a pool, gym, workshops library, dining room, and so forth.

What does it cost to get into this facility? Two options exist: either pay a full-price entry fee that is partially returnable to your estate upon your death or make a reduced-price nonrefundable entry-fee payment for your accommodations at this facility. For example, a two-bedroom apartment could cost $900,000.00 as an entry fee but upon the death, depending upon the facility and its contract, beneficiaries might receive anywhere from 50 percent to 90 percent of the entrance fee paid to the estate. Additionally, monthly fees amounting to several thousand dollars are charged to cover meals and facility amenities.

So what do you get for all these expenditures with this model of lifetime care? The answer is simple: peace of mind that you and/or your spouse or your parents will be cared for in a good facility for the rest of their days.

Other models also exist. For example, there are a number of facilities that identify themselves as life-care communities but all services while either on the same campus or nearby are "à la carte." Once again there is emotional security, but it may come at a significant price.

## Home Health Care

The CMS definition of home health care provides a useful starting point for discussion of this subject:

*Limited part-time or intermittent skilled nursing care and home health aide services, physical therapy, occupational therapy, speech-language therapy, medical social services, durable medical equipment (such as wheelchairs, hospital beds, oxygen, and walkers), medical supplies, and other services.*

There are several important issues with home health care services. The first is financial, that is, who pays for it. Theoretically, the government or some insurer should want to pay for home care as an alternative to nursing-home services. However, it is often the case that home health-care services, when offered in the same quantity and quality as nursing-home services, are more expensive. Additionally, while home-care services may be authorized for post-hospitalization care, rarely are they available from third-party payers for the long-term-type custodial care.

A second problem with home care is that of who is responsible on an hour-by-hour basis. For example, when my late wife was receiving home care for cancer, which meant oxygen, suction, IV antibiotics, and parenteral (tube) feeding, someone other than my wife needed to be responsible for running the equipment and administering the treatment. The home-care philosophy is to train a family member to provide the bulk of the coverage and oversight 24-7. Without the competent help of a family member or friend, home care is, in my judgment, merely a short-term solution that may be somewhat illusory. In other words, unless a family is wealthy enough to hire a dedicated and competent staff to provide in-home care, this is a poor alternative to the aforementioned options.

For those interested in home-care options, there is within the Medicare.gov website a tab on the left side titled "Find Home Health Care Services." As with the similar nursing-home tab (chapter 10 provides an extensive discussion about using this site), a consumer need only enter a location or zip code to bring up basic information about the home-care agencies in his or her area. I will illustrate this by using zip code 01060 (Northampton, Massachusetts) where I found a total of twenty-nine Medicare-certified agencies in the area. This information can be filtered by star ratings on two components: (1) quality of patient-care rating and (2) patient survey summary ratings. In this zip code, there were two facilities that received five stars in the quality rating and both were four star in the patient survey rating (there were no five-star patient ratings). However, there were a total of six agencies that received four stars in the patient survey rating category, and other than the two that were five star in quality, there were two others in the three- and three-and-a-half-star category and, amazingly enough, two others that received a one star for quality! Obviously patient or family perceptions may be quite different from that of the professionals.

As with the nursing-home site, tabs can be opened for more detailed information about quality and the patient survey results. What is most valuable with the quality data is not the overall star rating but the detailed statistical information from the quality measure categories of (1) managing daily activities, (2) managing pain and treating symptoms, (3) preventing harm, and (4) preventing unplanned hospital care. For example, under the Managing Pain and Treating Symptoms category, there are three measures: (1) how often patients had less pain when moving around, (2) how often patients' breathing improved, and (3) how often patients' wounds improved or healed after an operation. The data are presented in three columns. The first column is the particular home health-care agency's average in the category. The second column is the state average, and the third column is the national average.

As noted with the nursing home, data information is also a snapshot, and the careful consumer must do additional investigation. For example, with three minutes of Internet digging, I learned that one of the home-care companies I might theoretically be considering was publicly traded on NASDAQ, and in April 2014, the company signed an agreement with the US government to pay $150 million to "resolve allegations that they violated the False Claims Act by submitting false home healthcare billings to the Medicare program." Additionally, as part of their settlement with the government, the company is bound to the terms of a corporate integrity agreement that is designed to insure compliance with all federal rules and regulations. So the bad news is that this company allegedly provided unnecessary services to Medicare patients, but for those living in zip code 01060, it is important to recognize that violations occurred in Massachusetts. Additionally, the good news is that there will be plenty of government-directed organizational oversight, and according to the most current data, the company is doing a good job! However, the work for the consumer remains in comparing company no. one with company no. two.

## A Final Word about Aging in Place

The US Centers for Disease Control and Prevention defines aging in place as "the ability to live in one's home and community safely, independently, and comfortably, regardless of age, income or ability level." Great idea. But is it always possible? Certainly if you have enough financial and perhaps emotional resources! I know people who stay in their home or apartment with caregivers, drivers, cooks, and so forth. But realistically things do change—even when you do nothing. For example, I have many friends who are selling their homes and downsizing and oftentimes moving into condo communities. Why do they do this when they *love* their homes? Simply because they are tired of dealing with the myriad challenges of home ownership such as cutting grass, repairing fences or gates, shoveling snow, or cleaning a pool. While people can be hired for any of these functions, the costs sometimes get high, particularly for those on fixed retirement incomes.

Other issues with *aging in place* are what happens if a person gets sick and needs nursing home or rehab care? Or if one can no longer drive and lives in the suburbs or a city without good public transportation? Or if a person's husband or wife needs nursing home care but they are still well. While there are no simple answers, many people, particularly those who are upper middle class, or have saved enough money, or perhaps have a windfall from the sale of a house, turn to a CCRC with its *guarantee* of lifetime care.

# CHAPTER 5

## The Basics of Paying for Nursing-Home Care

### Introduction

The issue is a simple one: Who is going to pay the nursing-home bill that is fast approaching $100,000.00? Despite myriad misconceptions, Medicare usually won't. Medicaid might if the resident is poor enough. In the end, the family may be left holding the bag. This chapter provides an overview of the options for financing nursing-home care and identifies what steps a family could take to clarify eligibility for public payment for care. Additionally, in the last major section of this chapter, I sort through many of the confusing questions that are most often raised by consumers about long-term care.

### Medicare (And a Bit of History)

Elderly people and their families often believe that Medicare will pay most nursing-home bills. The casual statements of politicians periodically reinforce this misconception. For example, from a historical standpoint, after President Ronald Reagan signed the Catastrophic Coverage Act of 1988, the Democratic senator from Texas and sponsor of the bill, Lloyd Bentsen, said, "What we're doing is saying to the elderly that the nightmare that you feared so much if you have a catastrophic illness you're going to have your life savings wiped out...that's going to be taken care of." Senator Bentsen was not alone in sending out mixed messages about this amendment to the Medicare legislation. Senator John Chafee, Republican from Rhode Island, stated, "This vote will give the elderly long-overdue peace of mind." And Senator Barbara Mikulski, Democrat from Maryland, added that the bill would prevent the elderly from going into financial ruin and that the bill was "greatly needed to shore up the safety net for seniors."

Despite these statements from politicians, this bill probably should have been called the "Election Year Acute Care Catastrophic Coverage Act." Such a label would have been more accurate since the primary focus of the bill was on insuring the elderly against being wiped out by long hospital stays.

The unfortunate reality is that over the years Medicare has, with limited exceptions, provided minimal nursing-home coverage except for rehabilitative services.

Medicare is structured as a two-part health-insurance system for people older than sixty-five and for other people, regardless of age, who have certain disabilities or chronic diseases, such as end-stage renal disease. The first part of the system, called "Part A," is essentially a hospital insurance program. Like any other hospital insurance program, it collects premiums, sets limits on what it will pay, has deductibles, and has all kinds of rules. For example, Medicare covers semiprivate accommodations, meals (including special diets), laboratory and X-ray testing, operating-room charges, and drug costs while in the hospital. Examples of costs that are not covered are telephone charges or private-duty nurses a patient or family orders for convenience or peace of mind.

The confusion about the Medicare and nursing-home coverage exists because the government, as a prudent buyer of health services, decided that, in some instances, it would save money by paying for the equivalent of hospital services in a less expensive facility, that is, in a skilled-nursing home. So Medicare pays for all of the part up to one hundred days in a skilled-nursing facility if certain requirements are met. The two prime requirements are the following: (1) the Medicare beneficiary is transferred to a nursing home subsequent to a recent hospital stay for the same condition that hospital treating and (2) the services to be provided in the nursing home are of a skilled nature. These requirements also meant that Medicare will not pay for maintenance and custodial care, which is what most of nursing-home care is all about.

Another and perhaps simpler way of looking at this is that, at the present time, Medicare allows skilled-nursing facilities to function as an extension of a hospital, that is, providing the same care a patient would receive in a hospital at a lower price.

However, the person who is transferred to a skilled home for rehabilitation under Medicare does not get a free ride for his or her time in the skilled-nursing home. Specifically, Medicare pays in full for the first twenty days, but from day twenty-one through day one hundred, the patient is required to pay $164.50 per day. After day one hundred, the resident is responsible for the total bill.

If a person is in a skilled-nursing home under Medicare, it most often means that he or she is undergoing rehabilitation post some serious medical incidents such as a stroke or heart attack or subsequent to surgery such as a hip replacement. Recently I visited such a nursing-home facility in Olympia, Washington, where I observed an eighteen-hundred-square-foot rehabilitation facility that was bright and staffed with energetic therapists. What particularly impressed me was the space devoted to activities of daily living, including a full kitchen, bedroom, bathroom, and area for washing and drying clothes. The goal of this unit was returning people to their homes with the regained or adaptive skills to be successful in their own environments.

In a different nursing home, I saw another example of helping patients reintegrate to a regular lifestyle. In the rehab area, that nursing home had a convertible automobile (top down and stripped of the engine). This non-drivable auto had been recycled as a *vehicle* to help patients practice the skills associated with getting into and out of a car.

All the rehab patients I observed were relearning the tasks associated with activities of daily living. As they were rebuilding their strength and skills, they were also learning how to navigate around their limitations. One therapist noted to me that sometimes her job is merely confidence building while at other times finding adaptive devices to help the patients navigate their homes more easily.

In some instances therapists worked with local contractors on construction projects to make a house or apartment more user friendly. At several nursing homes that I visited, the staff also conducted home visits along with the patients and their families in order to assess any potential difficult situations at home that needed resolution before the final move back home.

In summary, what is important to recognize is that while Medicare is the primary payer of hospital bills for the elderly and rehabilitation services for certain diagnoses for limited periods of time, it cannot be looked to as a source of insurance for custodial long-term care.

On the other hand, Medicaid, the health program for the impoverished or medically needy, will pick up the custodial-care bill for a patient who qualifies. The next section examines the role of Medicaid in paying for nursing-home care.

## Medicaid

One of my all-time favorite popular articles on Medicaid was published in the October 3, 1988, issue of *People* magazine. It told the story of Celia Goldie, a ninety-year-old woman who moved from her condo on Chicago's North Shore to a nursing home in suburban Skokie. The article pointed out that prior to moving into the nursing home, Mrs. Goldie, a widow with a married and a devoted son, had been living on financial thin ice. Her $25,000 in savings had been depleted by expenses for aides and housekeepers who were needed after she had a heart attack and stroke three years earlier, and her $597 monthly Social Security income did not cover her $700 mortgage and maintenance payments nor her grocery bills and the salary of her $160-per-week companion. The move to the nursing home meant an end to her crisis and the subsidy provided by her son, because once she was eligible for Medicaid, it would pay for most of her nursing-home costs.

Mrs. Goldie's story is not significantly different from those of hundreds of thousands of others who live middle-class lives but find themselves unable to afford the ever-escalating costs of nursing-home care. Fortunately, the solution is the Medicaid program.

Medicaid is not to be confused with Medicare. As explained in the previous section, Medicare is a federal hospital and medical-insurance program tied to the Social Security system. Medicaid is a joint state and federal program that provides funding for health services for the needy. The framework for Medicaid comes from a set of federal regulations that were described by Supreme Court justice Lewis Powell as Byzantine. Another federal judge described the statute as being "unintelligible to the uninitiated." While the federal government provides the framework, it is up to the states to make the decisions about the provision of services and eligibility. The result of all this *flexibility* is, as already noted regarding the Medicare program, that there is considerable variability among the states.

At the level of nursing-home owners and managers, the variability comes in terms of how much the state Medicaid program will reimburse the home for a day of care for a Medicaid recipient. In fact, there is no uniformity of payment throughout the country, and the various systems used such as RUG-IV or other case mix systems are not only irrelevant for consumers but also changing in the near future. Since federal law prohibits the family or the resident from supplementing the Medicaid payment, whatever the nursing home receives as reimbursement from the state Medicaid program becomes the home's only revenue for the Medicaid beneficiary—regardless of the cost (salaries, supplies, services, and overhead).

From the perspective of the long-term resident or the potential resident of a nursing home, the threshold question is whether they are eligible for Medicaid. Determinations about eligibility for Medicaid-covered nursing-home care are not determinations made by anyone at a nursing home, but rather by a local governmental office after gathering information from an applicant about assets and income. In terms of assets, the Medicaid system generally asks about the prospective resident's real and personal property, and if it exceeds the specified maximum, the person must "spend down" to the limit before becoming eligible. In other words, applicants must deplete their own resources before the government will pay. In terms of income, the income must be used first to offset the nursing-home bill before the Medicaid program will pay.

For an unfortunate number of people, a lifetime of scrimping and saving for the "golden years" winds up being spent in less than a year in a nursing home. Some families wishing to minimize the risk of losing a lifetime's worth of savings to a long-term-care facility have turned to the option of long-term-care insurance. In the final section of this chapter, I shall explore the ins and outs of this third financing option.

## Long-Term-Care Insurance

On a national basis, approximately one-third of the spending in nursing homes came from private pay sources, that is, residents, members of their families, or long-term-care insurance. And as of 2013, only 10 percent of Americans have long-term-care insurance of any type. Unfortunately, for both the elderly and nursing-home operators, this insurance product does not solve many problems—indeed, for the most part, it confuses matters.

To understand the problem with long-term-care insurance, it helps to recognize first that insurance companies are not in business to provide charity; they are financial institutions interested in profits, and those profits are generated by collecting premiums and investing those premiums, but profits are reduced when insured events occur. To avoid too many high-priced payoffs, they must charge high-enough premiums, insure large-enough populations, and set payoff conditions. Basically, the insurance company is betting *against* certain events happening, and the insured is betting that these events *will* occur.

In the case of long-term-care insurance, the "event" that the company must be concerned about is an extremely expensive one. While the average annual nursing-home bill is in excess of $89,000, it should also be remembered that there are huge variations between states. For example, in a 2017 Lincoln Financial Group study on the annual costs of long-term care, it was reported that Texas, Missouri, and Louisiana were the three least expensive states for nursing-home care with respective costs of $56,210, $59,860, and $60,955. On the other hand, the most expensive states for someone to occupy a nursing-home bed (in a semiprivate room) are Alaska at $167,535, Connecticut at $155,490, and its neighbor Massachusetts at $143,080.

In light of these potentially devastating bills for a person who pays privately, the issue is simply what should one do: to buy or not to buy that is the question! Unfortunately there is no simple answer. The Internet offers over one million sites that provide discussions about the pros and cons of long-term-care insurance. From my perspective the pros are clear: an insurance company will pay all or part of the bill if you wind up in a nursing home or need other services. The cons are equally clear: such insurance can be quite expensive.

The Mutual of Omaha website is particularly useful because it offers a calculator as well as average prices per state. For example, it lists the cost of a semiprivate room in the state of Florida as $94,370.75 per year. It then presents a calculator, and using it I learned that a single man who is seventy-seven years old and wants a benefit amount of $7,000.00 per month ($84,000 per year), which would last for three years, would initially be paying $11,256 per year for the insurance. The website calculates the same benefit in Massachusetts, where a semiprivate room costs $138,345.95 per year, as a premium of $1,303.00 per month or $15,690 per year.

One highly respected certified public accountant (who became an insurance broker) suggested to me that long-term-care insurance is really a way to protect part of one's estate. However, he did add that if someone had enough money, that is, well over $3 million, long-term-care insurance wasn't really necessary. The bottom line is indeed the bottom line. And it's a gamble no matter what you do!

## Sorting through the Confusion

While some of the material on Medicare and Medicaid may seem technical, what is most relevant to know is that some nursing homes will only accept private-pay residents, others have waiting lists that may have differential priorities, and some may have hidden charges for family members. The key for any family is taking the time to read the contract that will have to be signed before admission. (Appendices 3 and 4 are critical preparation before reading any nursing-home contract.)

When reviewing a contract, certain issues need to be clarified such as if there are incidental expenses for laundry, television cable charges, personal grooming (beauty/barber shops), special requests such as for a particular brand of toothpaste, or transportation charges to medical appointments. Ambiguity is the enemy in any contract—the consumer needs to read carefully and question wisely.

## Key Questions (And Answers)

Below I have presented fourteen questions (and answers) that many consumers need answered immediately before they can even consider the possibility of a nursing home. These are merely the issues to begin a dialogue, not the end of the discussion! I fully recognize that some of this information may have been covered earlier in the text, but for some the Q&A approach may prove to be more useful.

### 1. How do I get on Medicaid?

Medicaid, a state-federal program, has numerous rules, and these rules vary from state to state. For example, some states have residency rules that require an applicant to live in that state for defined period of time, for example, six months, before being eligible for Medicaid. Other states allow a person to apply for Medicaid the moment he or she sets foot in the state. Is this important? Certainly. What if your parent lives in another state and is eligible for Medicaid in his or her home state? Again, rules vary by states—in some instances it is instant admission to Medicaid, and in other instances there are waiting periods. For example, when my sister needed a nursing home, she moved from her house in Florida into a Massachusetts nursing home and, because of her financial situation, immediately qualified for Medicaid despite the fact that she never had lived a single day in her life in Massachusetts. If the situation had been reversed, that is, she moved from Massachusetts to Florida, she would have had a six-month waiting period. An interesting question is what exactly happens to people without resources during such a waiting period.

With regard to eligibility, there are basically two tests: income and assets. If a person's income from all sources or assets exceeds certain limits, then eligibility isn't granted. To know the rules in each state, it is easiest to speak to a nursing-home admissions coordinator or social worker. Another option is speaking with the local Medicaid office. However, always remember that advisory opinions do not count—only the official state determination is significant.

**2. Will Medicare pay for my nursing-home care?**

Yes and no. Let's start with the "no." Medicare, the federal health-insurance program, will not pay for long-term custodial care. It is possible that you may have heard some stories about Medicare paying for such care in the past. These stories are true. However, those payments occurred because of a loophole in the Medicare-program regulations several decades ago. Once the loophole was discovered, it was closed, and those people whose custodial care was covered by Medicare were shifted back to either Medicaid or private-pay status.

The "yes" is that when the care at the nursing home is technically related to a hospital stay, Medicare pays. Essentially the federal government is using the nursing home as a cheaper alternative to the hospital, but the concept is that the patient will have a limited-time-duration stay. Typically nursing homes that have both rehab and custodial patients provide rooms for the two types of residents in separate sections of a building. For example, in one place I visited, the second floor was devoted to short-term rehabilitation where most patients were covered by Medicare. The other floors of the building housed the long-term-care residents who have essentially made the nursing home their domicile (indeed many vote from the home). These residents were covered by Medicaid or paid privately.

Essentially then the "patients" tend to get Medicare coverage (assuming they meet Medicare eligibility) and the "residents" pay either privately or through the state Medicaid program.

**3. Who will be my doctor at the nursing home?**

Theoretically the doctor any individual uses before he or she goes into a nursing home can continue with him or her after he or she is admitted to the home. Practically it oftentimes does not work that way because sometimes the nursing home is in a different community and often one's primary-care physician simply does not do visits at nursing homes. More commonly, only a handful of physicians take care of the residents in nursing homes. These are usually MDs who have an interest in geriatrics and have committed a percentage of their practice to nursing-home residents.

In the best of situations, a nursing home will employ a full-time physician or geriatric nurse practitioner who will be available as an in-house practitioner. Such arrangements are most likely to be found in government or large nonprofit nursing homes. Even if such an arrangement exists, it is possible to continue using the primary-care MD a person had before nursing-home admittance. Indeed, federal and state laws insure that the patient has freedom of choice in physician selection.

**4. What happens if I need specialty medical care?**

In the best of situations such as at the Miami Jewish Home and Hospital (now known as the Miami Jewish Health System), the nursing home maintains its own specialty clinic. For example, in Miami the clinic staff included specialists in numerous specialties including dermatology, orthopedics, dentistry, ophthalmology, optometry, and psychiatry. The more typical facility has a list of specialists who are regularly used by residents and are best able to provide care to the frail elderly. However, a resident is always free to select his or her own specialist. One problem though is that of actually accessing the out-of-facility specialist. For example, how is transportation going to be arranged? And will it be necessary for the resident to be accompanied by an aide at the specialist's office? If so, who will accompany the resident, and, in some instances, who will pay for that aide?

Illustrative of this situation was my late sister's experiences. When she needed to leave the nursing home for an appointment, arrangements had to be made with either the nursing home's transportation office or the local handicapped/elderly transit authority to both take her to the doctor and pick her up. She also needed to have an aide with her on these trips.

**5. What happens with my prescription medication?**

Most residents do not have any issues with prescription medications that are typically paid for by Medicare part D or Medicaid. In some cases the nursing home may be obliged to use an equivalent drug to the one that had been taken. This is because the different Medicare payers have each established formularies, that is, drugs they use for specific conditions. Generally though this is not a major problem.

However, what may be a problem is the abuse of patients by medication. Various reports indicate that almost one-fifth of residents in nursing homes are receiving antipsychotic medications. What is astounding is that there are huge variations between states. For example, in the second quarter of 2014, Texas and Maine reported that at least 25 percent of their nursing-home residents were receiving antipsychotic drugs while Hawaii reported 9.1 percent, Michigan reported 13.4 percent, and New Jersey reported 14.2 percent. But even within states there are variations. Illustrative of this is the fact that in 2017, South Carolina was ranked eighteenth in the country for antipsychotic drug use with a rate of 14.6 percent, but in a December 4, 2017, article in the *Island Packet* (a local Hilton Head, South Carolina, newspaper), the reporter Maggie Angst found that one of the nursing homes in the area had 28.6 percent of residents on antipsychotic drugs while a second home had 24.1 percent of its residents on these drugs. In both instances these particular homes would have been at the top of the national list. The reasons for this are typically twofold: First, the nursing home wants to keep certain residents tranquilized such as those whose Alzheimer's disease causes them to act out or be aggressive. A second, albeit cynical, reason is to increase reimbursement fees to the home. For the careful consumer, it is imperative to be sensitive and alert to this potential abuse and avoid any such homes.

**6. Can I continue to use my nonprescription medications?**

Nursing homes stock the most commonly used over-the-counter medications, and they are provided to the resident as part of the room rate. In general nursing homes are not keen on residents self-medicating.

**7. Can I furnish my own room?**

There is no standard answer to this question. I have visited homes that prohibit residents from bringing anything other than some photos into the room. In those instances the rooms are oftentimes nicely furnished, but the nursing homes have made a policy decision to keep the facility looking in a particular manner. Many homes, however, allow residents to bring in items from home. I have seen rooms furnished with dressers and night tables brought from home and often a favored chair. Pictures on the wall or a homey bedspread makes all the difference. My sister decorated her standard nursing-home room with family photos, plants, candy jars, a deck chair for visitors, a TV and VCR, an afghan bedspread that our mother had crocheted, and several stuffed animals. The net effect was that of a cozy studio apartment rather than a sterile residential facility room without personality.

**8. Can I have a private room?**

Not all facilities have private rooms, and when they do, they are typically reserved for private paying residents. If this is an issue that is important, then it may be necessary to scout around to find a home with a good proportion of private rooms and one that will allocate the room in a nonfinancially discriminatory manner. In one nursing home that I visited, there were a total of 150 rooms, 100 of which were private. The other 50 were semiprivate. In that particular home, 80 percent of the residents were on Medicaid, so from a purely statistical perspective, some of them had private rooms. In practice more than 50 percent of the Medicaid residents were indeed in private rooms.

**9. Does a private room mean better care?**

No. The quality of care that a person receives is generally unrelated to his or her accommodations. Regardless of the source of payment for a resident's care, every resident has the exact same rights to care, dignity, and services.

**10. Can I leave the nursing home for hospitalizations or vacations with my friends and family?**

The term used in answer to this question is "bed hold." The issue for the nursing home is similar to that of a hotel, that is, the home wants to keep its beds full and the revenue coming in for those beds. Complicating the equation though is that states have the authority to set "bed-hold" policies for nursing homes, and there is significant variation among the states. Additionally bed-hold policy is different for hospital transfers or therapeutic leaves. For example, Colorado does not provide any nursing-home leave days for hospitalization. The implication of the Colorado policy is that it is possible that once a person is transferred from a nursing home to a hospital, his or her bed will be filled and unavailable upon his or her return. By contrast Massachusetts Medicaid pays a nursing home for up to ten days to hold the bed for a hospitalized Medicaid recipient.

A different aspect of bed-hold policies becomes an issue when a resident wants to take a vacation from the nursing home. For example, assume there is a family gathering in another state and the resident is able to attend, participate, and return, but it will take four days. As with the hospitalization rules, there is significant variance among the states on these therapeutic leaves ranging from those states that will not hold the bed to those states that allow more than eighteen days of leave per year.

It is imperative that potential residents and their families examine the bed-hold policies of the homes they are considering for a move.

**11. Once I am in a nursing home, am I stuck there for life?**

Absolutely not! A resident is exactly that, a resident. A nursing home is a home, not a prison! If the resident and/or the resident's family want to leave, then they simply give notice and leave. If the resident is unhappy with the home, then the resident and/or family should take steps to either remedy the problem or transfer the resident to another home. In some states there are state-run programs to get residents out of the nursing-home facility and into a home or homelike setting.

For example, several states have a nursing-home transition program that allows nursing-home residents to leave the facility and be treated in a family member's home or an assisted-living center with some state-funded services.

**12. If I have complaints about my nursing-home care, what can I do?**

The vast majority of nursing home staff and management want to run good facilities and insure that their residents are cared for properly. Occasionally there are caregivers who behave badly and care is subpar. In those instances the residents have a variety of options. First, they can follow the institution's own procedure for resolving such problems such as complaining to the management or the residents' council. Another option is contacting the local nursing-home ombudsman—every state has an ombudsman program to deal with resident issues. A third route is complaining to the state agency that has oversight of nursing home. This usually triggers a state-government complaint survey (which nursing homes do not like). Finally, a lawyer can be engaged to represent the resident.

Some organizations have 1-800 hotlines for patients to register problems and complaints. My absolute favorite program is one that we have at all the Extendicare nursing homes called the Guardian Angel Program. This program assigned every resident in a nursing home a nonclinical staff member of the nursing home to be a guardian angel, that is, to be that resident's friend and advocate. Such a program both empowers the resident and mitigates problems.

**13. What is the impact of "Obamacare" on nursing home (long-term care) and Trump's potential dismantling of that program?**

For new residents the impact is essentially insignificant. On the other hand, there may be subtle impacts on the care that is received if the elderly resident needs some additional services such as speech, occupational, or rehabilitation therapy.

**14. What is the best way to insure that a nursing-home resident gets good care?**

Recently I was talking with a retired public-school teacher whose mother is a resident of an outstanding nursing home in the suburbs of a major metropolitan center. I asked him how was the day-to-day care for his mom. He replied that it was great and that the staff were completely dedicated to his elderly mother. I then continued with the following question: How often do you visit your mom and typically how long are your visits? The answer: every day and usually three to four hours.

In my opinion, while this man was in the top 1 percent of devoted children, he also demonstrated the fact that those residents who have regular visitors, who not only visit but watch over the process of care for their loved ones, frequently get better care than the many residents who rarely or never have visitors.

# CHAPTER 6

# Organizational Issues

**[NOTE: While this section primarily focuses on nursing homes, the information provided also applies to other segments of the long-term-care industry.]**

## Nursing-Home Ownership: Implications

Understanding who owns the 15,640 nursing homes in the United States (as of 2014) and the implications of that ownership is both difficult and important for consumers. Approximately 10,913 (70 percent) homes are operated as for-profit businesses by individuals, closely held corporations, or publicly traded companies. There are also 3,756 not-for-profit homes and 971 government homes.

If a consumer is interested in considering a private home, it is useful to figure out who owns the home and what the owner's reputation is. For example, in the case of the Rehabilitation Center at Hollywood Hills described in the preface, with a modicum of digging, anyone could learn that the parent company of the nursing home was a hospital owned by several partners who had a significant history of problems with the US Department of Justice. These problems resulted in multimillion settlements with the government. As of 2017 one partner is in the Miami Federal Detention Center awaiting trial on a billion dollar Medicare fraud charge; a second partner has had multiple scrapes with the Department of Justice, while a third partner was part of a multimillion settlement with the Department of Justice over health-care-related issues. Would that set up a red flag? It would for me!

Figuring out ownership takes some research. There are dozens of large chains that own over one hundred homes and numerous smaller chains that own ten or more homes. The fact that a home is owned privately and is a for-profit entity should cause any consumer to investigate further but not necessarily dismiss the home from consideration. There are many other important issues that should be considered before making a decision. One of the good things about the nursing-home chains that are on a stock exchange is that there are numerous public documents about the company. Consider Genesis—a company that owns (according to its website) 450 skilled nursing facilities in thirty states as well as a rehabilitation-therapy operation that services in the neighborhood of seventeen hundred locations. As a public company, they have numerous filing requirements, and from these documents easily accessible, one can learn a good deal about the financial health of the company and in some instances specific homes. Press releases as well as Yahoo's finance website are quite useful. For example, on December 5, 2017, I searched Yahoo's site and learned that the Genesis stock was selling at seventy-nine cents a share, down from $4.53 at the beginning of January 2017, and way down from historic highs. The site has recommendations as well as conversations. I am not a stock analyst, but their unfortunate financial condition might again set up some red flags. These issues will be discussed later in this book.

The governmental sector of approximately twelve hundred nursing homes is certainly a much clearer group. For example, in Northampton, Massachusetts, a college town of twenty-five thousand people, there is one government-owned nursing home that is a forty-four-bed facility owned by the US Department of Veteran's Affairs. Until a decade ago, there was also an excellent nursing home owned by and operated for residents of the county. A private, for-profit company home now owns that facility.

About eight miles south of Northampton is the Soldiers' Home in Holyoke, Massachusetts. This excellent facility is owned by the state of

Massachusetts and provides long-term care to veterans at a modest per diem rate to the family. The Holyoke home is one of two in the state (the other is in Chelsea). There is often at least one similar home in each state, and information on these places can be found out from the Department of Veterans Affairs.

The third category of ownership, which accounts for approximately thirty-seven hundred facilities, is the voluntary, not-for-profit home. These homes, which typically have charitable or religious roots, are organized so that no part of the home's net earnings operates to benefit any private shareholders. Various levels of government have struck a bargain with these organizations so that if they act in and for the public good by eschewing the personal (as opposed to organizational) benefits of profit, the organization will be exempt from federal income taxes as well as state and local real-estate and sales taxes.

At this point I should note that even in the not-for-profit sector, there can be some consumer confusion that comes from two directions. First, there have been a number of organizations that started out as for-profit facilities and converted part of their operation, typically the operational nursing home, into a 501(c)3 nursing home, that is, the Internal Revenue Service's designation of not-for-profit charitable organizations. The original for-profit entity then sets up a for-profit management company, which contracts with the nursing home to run the facility. Sometimes as part of the operation, the original group of owners still owns the all the physical property and leases the land and building to the nursing home.

Why do this? There are many reasons related to taxes, liability, and resident and family perception. Another issue with the not-for-profits is, in my personal opinion, the outrageous salaries some of the executives are getting from their operations—when the CEO of a nonprofit earns millions of dollars, more than the executives of many of America's largest corporations do! These institutions are public trusts; taking charitable money and the overreaching by executives mean that less money is available for residents.

However, when it comes to the nonprofits and government homes, the answer is fairly clear, as is the recourse of the consumer. Having trouble with the nursing home run by local government, call your local politician. Having problems with the home owned by the Masons, the Presbyterians, the Lutherans, or the local Jewish community—call a board member or bigwig in the church. But whom are you going to call when a private equity firm or group of investors in Washington, New York, or Abu Dubai owns the home?

The nonprofit situation also potentially benefits the nursing home's residents in a variety of ways. First, the dollars that a home would have to pay in taxes are now freed up to provide for more staff and programs. Second, charitable or religiously rooted not-for-profit homes frequently are involved in extensive fund-raising projects that provide additional sources of revenue. Illustrative of this fund-raising is one home that I visited where the women's club generates close to $30,000 each year at a donor dinner and another group raises in excess of $10,000 at an annual tennis and golf tournament. At the Miami Jewish Home, my staff of nine people raised several million dollars per year. And those extra dollars translated into more staff and programs.

The nonprofit arrangement also offers a double quid pro quo for the donor: giving to a good cause and a tax deduction for the gift. As tax laws change over time, there is an open question whether such deductions will remain in the future. Regardless of tax laws, many of the excellent not-for-profit homes have significant endowments, typically isolated from operation funds, in foundations dedicated to servicing the elderly. The funds from these foundations are absolutely invaluable in providing the money necessary for excellent care. Third, perhaps because of their charitable roots, not-for-profit homes—and to some extent federally owned homes (particularly Veterans Administration nursing facilities)—do an outstanding job in developing vibrant volunteer programs.

Indeed, active volunteers play an invaluable role in maintaining contact between the resident and the community, and a secondary but real role in augmenting a nursing home's staff. During my visits to nursing homes, I have seen volunteers reading to residents, leading exercise and sing-along groups, helping the frail elderly write letters or even biographies, and taking people out for a snack or a ride (in one case, in a volunteer's Rolls-Royce). Volunteers come in all sizes and ages. One of the most touching programs I observed involved over a dozen teenagers at a summer camp who devoted one morning per week visiting residents at a nearby nursing home.

From a manpower perspective, the tens of thousands of hours that volunteers spend in a nursing home can provide the equivalent of having a large staff. In Miami I estimated that the volunteers augmented my staff by an average of several dozen people per week.

It should be noted that a fair number of for-profit facilities, particularly those grounded in their communities, also offer vibrant volunteer programs that enhance the life of residents.

Another important aspect of the not-for-profit home is the philosophical orientation, which means that the "profits" (i.e., any excess of income over expenses) are to be reinvested in the home. In practice, many not-for-profits do not generate significant profits because they are continuously spending their money on staff or on items that a for-profit home is unlikely to purchase, such as vehicles to transport residents to outside activities.

The clearest manifestation of the differences among the not-for-profit, government, and for-profit facilities is seen in the staffing. For example, in 2014, a report (GAO-16-700) presented a table that showed the average nursing time per day by home ownership. For-profit nursing home reported three hours and fifty-three minutes of overall nursing time per resident day compared with four hours and seven minutes for nonprofit homes and three hours and fifty-nine minutes for government-owned homes. While fourteen minutes more per day for the nonprofit (compared to the for-profit home) may sound insignificant, that also means more than an hour and a half of nursing care per week. And that may mean the difference between adequate care and perhaps better and more tender care! Incidentally of those fourteen extra minutes per resident day, four minutes were accounted for by registered nurses. Once again, that is approximately half an hour more RN care per week—typically in critical supervision.

Unfortunately nursing homes also have high staff turnover rates that make it exceedingly important to realize the importance of a home's staffing. Numerous studies conclude that the for-profit homes often have lower staffing ratios than those of not-for-profit homes. As I looked at homes during my various field visits, I saw the confirmation of this data on a local basis. The private homes tended to have between 10 and 15 percent fewer staff members than the not-for-profit ones. Although some of this staffing difference occurs in the secondary administrative areas, the greatest part of the difference can typically be found in the number of nursing and therapeutic service staff in the not-for-profit home.

Finally, the not-for-profit (and to some extent the government-owned) homes have a built-in community watchdog group, usually called the board of directors or the board of trustees. Such a group, frequently comprising prominent citizens, has the responsibility for overseeing the home's operations. When I wrote *Choosing a Nursing Home*, I spoke to then president of the board of directors of the Riverview Center for Jewish Seniors in Pittsburgh. His work for Riverview was not confined to board meetings and telephone conversations. Indeed, when I made an unannounced visit to his Squirrel Hill store on a busy Thursday night, he immediately dropped what he was doing, took me into his back office, and proceeded to talk knowledgeably and at length about the Pittsburgh nursing-home scene. In the years since that visit, I have had the opportunity to work with boards from across the country. The same enthusiasm I first saw with that gentleman I have now seen repeated thousands of other times in hundreds of places. The gift these people provide in most instances translates into high-quality care. What these individuals also provide is direction, oversight, and the crucial link back to the community.

The importance of the ownership issue was superbly illustrated in an article that was written by Jordan Rau (with contributions from Elizabeth Lucas) and originally published on December 31, 2017, by *Kaiser Health News*. Titled "Care Suffers as More Nursing Homes Feed Money into Corporate Webs," the article points out the implications of nursing homes "contracting out" critical services to third parties. The central issue that emerges from this article is how do consumers find out what is truly going on with any given nursing home. Below, with the permission of the *Kaiser Health News*, I have reproduced Jordan Rau's important article in entirety:

***Care Suffers as More Nursing Homes Feed Money into Corporate Webs***

*By **Jordan Rau** DECEMBER 31, 2017*

*MEMPHIS, Tenn.—When one of Martha Jane Pierce's sons peeled back the white sock that had been covering his 82-year-old mother's right foot for a month, he discovered rotting flesh.*

*"It looked like a piece of black charcoal" and smelled "like death," her daughter Cindy Hatfield later testified. After Pierce, a patient at a Memphis nursing home, was transferred to a hospital, a surgeon had to amputate much of her leg.*

*One explanation for Pierce's lackluster care, according to financial records and testimony in a lawsuit brought by the Pierce family, is that her nursing home, Allenbrooke Nursing and Rehabilitation Center, appeared to be severely underfunded at the time, with a $2 million deficit on its books in 2009 and a scarcity of nurses and aides. "Sometimes we'd be short of diapers, sheets, linens," one nurse testified.*

*That same year, $2.8 million of the facility's $12 million in operating expenses went to a constellation of corporations controlled by two Long Island accountants who, court records show, owned Allenbrooke and 32 other nursing homes. The homes paid the men's other companies to provide physical therapy, management, drugs and other services, from which the owners reaped profits, according to court records.*

*In what has become an increasingly common business arrangement, owners of nursing homes outsource a wide variety of goods and services to companies in which they have a financial interest or that they control. Nearly three-quarters of nursing homes in the United States—more than 11,000—have such business dealings, known as related party transactions, according to an analysis of nursing home financial records by Kaiser Health News. Some homes even contract out basic functions like management or rent their own building from a sister corporation, saying it is simply an efficient way of running their businesses and can help minimize taxes.*

*But these arrangements offer another advantage: Owners can establish highly favorable contracts in which their nursing homes pay more than they might in a competitive market. Owners then siphon off higher profits, which are not recorded on the nursing home's accounts.*

*The two Long Island men, Donald Denz and Norbert Bennett, and their families' trusts collected distributions totaling $40 million from their chain's $145 million in revenue over eight years—a 28 percent margin, according to the judge's findings of fact. In 2014 alone, Denz earned $13 million and Bennett made $12 million, principally from their nursing home companies, according to personal income tax filings presented in court.*

*Typical nursing home profits are "in the 3 to 4 percent range," said Bill Ulrich, a nursing home financial consultant.*

*In 2015, nursing homes paid related companies $11 billion, a tenth of their spending, according to financial disclosures the homes submitted to Medicare.*

*In California, the state auditor is examining related party transactions at another nursing home chain, Brius Healthcare Services. Rental prices to the chain's real estate entities were a third higher than rates paid by other for-profit nursing homes in the same counties, according to an analysis by the National Union of Healthcare Workers.*

*Such corporate webs bring owners a legal benefit, too: When a nursing home is sued, injured residents and their families have a much harder time collecting money from the related companies—the ones with the full coffers.*

*After the Pierce family won an initial verdict against the nursing home, Denz and Bennett appealed, and their lawyer, Craig Conley, said they would not discuss details of the case or their business while the appeal was pending.*

*"For more than a decade, Allenbrooke's caregivers have promoted the health, safety and welfare of their residents," Conley wrote in an email.*

*Dr. Michael Wasserman, the head of the management company for the Brius nursing homes, called corporate structures a "nonissue" and said, "What matters at the end of the day is what the care being delivered is about."*

*Networks of jointly owned limited liability corporations are fully legal and used widely by other businesses, such as restaurants and retailers. Nonprofit nursing homes sometimes use them as well. Owners can have more control over operations—and better allocate resources—if they own all the companies. In many cases, industry consultants say, a commonly owned company will charge a nursing home lower fees than an independent contractor might, leaving the chain with more resources.*

*"You don't want to pay for someone else to make money off of you," Ulrich said. "You want to retain that within your organization."*

*But a Kaiser Health News analysis of federal inspection and quality records reveals that nursing homes that outsource to related organizations tend to have significant shortcomings: They have fewer nurses and aides per patient, they have higher rates of patient injuries and unsafe practices, and they are the subject of complaints almost twice as often as independent homes.*

*"Almost every single one of these chains is doing the same thing," said Charlene Harrington, a professor emeritus of the School of Nursing at the University of California-San Francisco. "They're just pulling money away from staffing."*

***Early Signs of Trouble***

*Martha Jane Pierce moved to Allenbrooke in 2008 in the early stages of dementia. According to testimony in the family's lawsuit, her children often discovered her unwashed when they visited, with an uneaten, cold meal sitting beside her bed. Hatfield said in court that she had frequently found her mother's bed soaked in urine. The front desk was sometimes vacant, her brother Glenn Pierce testified.*

*"If you went in on the weekend, you'd be lucky to find one nurse there," he said in an interview.*

*After a stroke, Pierce became partly paralyzed and nonverbal, but the nursing home did not increase the attention she received, said Carey Acerra, one of Pierce's lawyers. When Pierce's children visited, they rarely saw aides reposition her in bed every two hours, the standard practice to prevent bedsores.*

*"Not having enough staffing, we can't—we weren't actually able to go and do that," one nurse, Cheryl Gatlin-Andrews, testified in a deposition.*

*KHN's analysis of federal inspection, staffing and financial records nationwide found shortcomings at other homes with similar corporate structures:*

> *Homes that did business with sister companies employed, on average, 8 percent fewer nurses and aides.*
>
> *As a group, these homes were 9 percent more likely to have hurt residents or put them in immediate jeopardy of harm, and amassed*

*53 validated complaints for every 1,000 beds, compared with the 32 per 1,000 that inspectors found credible at independent homes.*

*Homes with related companies were fined 22 percent more often for serious health violations than were independent homes, and penalties averaged $24,441—7 percent higher.*

*For-profit nursing homes employ these related corporations more frequently than nonprofits do, and have fared worse than independent for-profit homes in fines, complaints and staffing, the analysis found. Their fines averaged $25,345, which was 10 percent higher than fines for independent for-profits, and the homes received 24 percent more substantiated complaints from residents. Overall staffing was 4 percent lower than at independent for-profits.*

*Ernest Tosh, a plaintiffs' lawyer in Texas who helps other lawyers untangle nursing company finances, said owners often exerted control by setting tight budgets that restricted the number of nurses the homes could employ. Meanwhile, "money is siphoned out to these related parties," he said. "The cash flow gets really obscured through the related party transactions."*

*The American Health Care Association, which represents nursing homes, disputed any link between related businesses and poor care. "Our members strive to provide quality care at an affordable cost to every resident," the group said in a statement. "There will always be examples of exceptions, but those few do not represent the majority of our profession."*

**"Piercing the Corporate Veil"**

*The model of placing nursing homes and related businesses in separate limited liability corporations and partnerships has gained popularity as the industry has consolidated through purchases by publicly traded companies, private investors and private equity firms. A 2003 article in the Journal of Health Law encouraged owners to separate their nursing home business into detached entities to protect themselves if the government tried to recoup overpayments or if juries levied large negligence judgments.*

*"Holding the real estate in a separate real-property entity that leases the nursing home to the operating entity protects the assets by making the real*

*estate unavailable for collection by judgment creditors of the operating entity," the authors wrote. Such restructuring, they added, was probably not worth it just for "administrative simplicity."*

*In 2009, Harvard Medical School researchers found the practice had flourished among nursing homes in Texas, which they studied because of the availability of state data. Owners had also inserted additional corporations between them and their nursing homes, with many separated by three layers.*

*To bring related companies into a lawsuit, attorneys must persuade judges that all the companies were essentially acting as one entity and that the nursing home could not make its own decisions. Often that requires getting access to internal company documents and emails. Even harder is holding owners personally responsible for the actions of a corporation—known as "piercing the corporate veil."*

*At a 2012 Nashville conference for executives in the long-term health care industry, a presentation slide from nursing home attorneys titled "Pros of Complex Corporate Structure" stated: "Many plaintiffs' attorneys will never conduct corporate structure discovery because it's too expensive and time consuming." The presentation noted another advantage: "Financial statement in punitive damages phase shows less income and assets."*

*A lawyer in Alabama, Barry Walker, is still fighting an 11-year-old case against another nursing home then owned by Denz and Bennett, according to court records. Walker traced the ownership of Fairfield Nursing and Rehabilitation Center back to the men, but he said the judge had allowed him to introduce the ownership information only after the Alabama Supreme Court ordered him. That trial ended with a hung jury, and Walker said a subsequent judge had not let him present all the information to two other juries, and he dropped the men from the lawsuit. The home closed a few years ago but the case is still ongoing despite two mistrials.*

*"The former trial judge and the current trial judge quite frankly don't seem to understand piercing the corporate veil," he said. "My firm invested more in the case than we can ever hope to recover. Sometimes it's a matter of principle."*

*The complexity of the ownership in Pierce's case was a major reason it took six years to get to a trial, said Ken Connor, one of the lawyers for her family. "It requires a lot of digging to unearth what's really going on," he said. "Most lawyers can't afford to do that."*

*The research paid off in a rare result: In 2016, the jury issued a $30 million verdict for negligence, of which Denz and Bennett were personally liable for $20 million. The men's own tax returns bolstered the case against them. They claimed during trial they delegated daily responsibilities for residents to the home's administrators, but they reported on their tax returns that they "actively" participated in the management. The jury did not find the nursing home responsible for Pierce's death later in 2009.*

*The fight is not over. Denz and Bennett are appealing the verdict, the damages, their inclusion and the trial judge's decisions. They argue that Tennessee courts should not have jurisdiction over them since they spent little time in the state and neither was involved in the daily operations of the home or in setting staffing levels. Their lawyers said jurors should never have heard from nurses who hadn't cared directly for Pierce.*

*"No way did I oversee resident care issues," Bennett testified in a deposition.*

***Deficient in the End***

*Whoever was responsible for Pierce's care, her family had no doubt it was inadequate. Her son Bill Pierce was so horrified when he finally saw the wound on his mother's foot, he immediately insisted that she go to the hospital.*

*"The surgeon said he had never seen anything like it," Hatfield said in an interview. "He amputated 60 percent of the leg, above the knee."*

*After her amputation, Pierce returned to the nursing home because her family did not want to separate her from her husband, who was also there.*

*At the trial, the nursing home's lawyers argued that Pierce's leg had deteriorated not because of the infection but because her blood vessels had become damaged from a decline in circulation. The jury was unpersuaded after nurses and aides testified about how Allenbrooke would add staffing for state inspections while the rest of the time their pleas for more support went unheeded.*

*Workers also testified that supervisors had told them to fill in blanks in medical records regardless of accuracy. One example: Allenbrooke's records indicated that Pierce had eaten a full meal the day after she died.*

*Data journalist Elizabeth Lucas contributed to this report.*

*KHN's coverage related to aging and improving care of older adults is supported in part by The John A. Hartford Foundation.*

## Management Issues

Here allow me to begin with my conclusion. Excellent management and excellent nursing leadership are the two most crucial elements in quality nursing homes. I based this both on research (unpublished) that was conducted during the several years I chaired a committee examining these issues in a large sample of nursing homes and my own observations of visiting nursing homes for the past three decades. Indeed, if I were to search for a nursing home for a loved one, among the first group of questions that I would ask are: Who is the administrator? How long has he or she been here? And what is her/his background? I would also ask the same questions about the nursing director. Yellow (caution) flags would go up if I learned that either of these people has been there only a short while and red (danger) flags would fly if I found out that either of these positions had revolving-door incumbents.

The significance of the nursing-home administrator is that he or she is the person licensed by the state as the individual responsible for the day-to-day management of the nursing home. While state requirements for licensure vary, basically they include some combination of education in health-care administration and experience in the field, typically through a supervised apprenticeship program. Subsequently, there are continuing-education requirements necessary for continued licensure.

In nursing homes, to a far greater degree than in other health-care organizations such as hospitals, management plays a key role. The administrator's job is that of translating the federal and state rules and regulations as well as the policies of the owner or governing body into the operations of the home. Failure to do the job effectively might mean being fired by the board or owners, fined by the state, and in some instances criminally indicted by the government. For example, there are some states where receiving a poor review on a Medicaid survey has led to criminal charges being filed against the nursing home's administrator. On the other hand, I have seen numerous examples of administrators around the country who have made a difference in their nursing homes.

During my years of university teaching, I always emphasized that the nursing-home administrator was the individual with his or her hand figuratively on the organizational thermostat. By this metaphor I tried to reinforce the idea that an administrator could be the catalyst for an organization being more or less supportive and responsive to residents, families, and staff. Alternatively he or she could be the point person for a punitive and, indeed, unpleasant organization. Such is the significance of leadership!

A case in point is the Eden Alternative, a concept developed by William Thomas, MD, from upstate New York. The essence of Dr. Thomas's idea is that the nursing home must become a more humanized environment. He takes the name Eden from the biblical Garden of Eden and promotes changing the environment in a variety of ways but most importantly by introducing plants, birds, dogs, cats, and other animals into the nursing home. In a YouTube video about the Eden Alternative, a nursing-home administrator in Tioga, New York, speaks about how she convinced her board of directors to accept the changes associated with the Eden Alternative. Today there are more than three hundred nursing homes that are full-fledged Eden Alternative facilities and perhaps thousands more that have adapted some measures of the Eden approach. In most cases it is an administrator whose leadership turns an idea into a viable program.

Over the years I've seen many examples of how the vision of one person can make a difference such as the work of an administrator in St. Louis who raised $4,000 for a children's playground adjacent to his nursing home. His idea, now replicated elsewhere including some Extendicare homes, was to give grandchildren and children something to do when they visit the home. Like the Eden Alternative, his goal with the playground was to encourage a more congenial and homelike atmosphere for everyone. The second aspect that attracted my attention was that none of the staff members at that nursing home wore uniforms. As the administrator saw it, uniforms are barriers to both relationships and communications.

In his zest for providing a less institutional environment, this person also encouraged numerous programs, such as the use of the thousands of feet of wall space as a rotating art gallery, the development of an active gardening-therapy program, and sensory stimulation activities. The gardens also served as the setting for professional musicians who provided a public-concert series as well as for the annual one-day crafts show with a carnival and barbecue that brought the residents together with the community.

Eating is clearly a universal experience, and, to some extent, hosting people for a meal is also part of many of our more memorable experiences. Institutionalization should not eliminate that option, and I've been privileged to see many nursing homes that have small private dining rooms where residents could host such dinners. Indeed, I even hosted my own prenuptials dinner in the dining room of a nursing home.

Most managers inherit the physical facilities in which they work; however, some of them are able to transform them quite dramatically. In a visit to a home on Bainbridge Island, Washington, I visited two nursing homes that had redesigned the nursing stations with lowered desks and space under them so that wheelchair-bound residents could meet the staff at eye level. In another facility an outdoor patio was installed in the front under a front portico. The entire look of the nursing home was of a Pacific Northwest ski lodge, not a nursing home.

On a trip to Seattle, I visited the 150-bed Seattle Keiro, now known as Keiro Rehabilitation and Care, which opened in 1987 as a facility for the elderly Japanese community in the Pacific Northwest. Now in its third decade of operations, it is still a place where serenity hits you in the face as you walk toward its entrance off a residential street in a hilly section of Seattle, about a twenty-minute walk from downtown. This serenity comes from the sensitive architectural design of traditional Japanese gardens and a shrine-type entryway. Once inside the building, one easily feels the pulse of a busy place with considerable cultural sensitivities. On my first visit to the home in the early 1990s, I was struck by the signs throughout the home in Japanese and English and large cue cards for staff with the various essential words in Japanese and English, nowadays in additional languages.

Also, on that first visit, I observed activities including videotaped Japanese television programs and ikebana (flower-arranging) sessions. On the floors, the monotony of the hallways was broken up by a number of tokonomas-alcoves with hanging scrolls and traditional vases of flowers.

On a second visit several years ago, the floors still looked the same and many of the activities and volunteer programs continued as before; there were some important changes that illustrated the importance of good management. Obviously some of the simplest changes were responses to twenty-first-century technology. No longer do people have to watch videotaped programs from Japan; rather certain TVs are always tuned to the Japanese TV channels brought in by satellite and cable. The home's name, Keiro, means, "respected elder," and it certainly lived up to its name.

Nothing though is more important than the attitude of management toward the residents. Two examples. First I am reminded of an incident that I witnessed a number of years ago on a warm summer evening in the lobby of nursing home in Western Massachusetts. It was about 6:00 p.m., and the home's newly appointed director was heading through the lobby to take a walk before a 6:30 p.m. board dinner scheduled for the auditorium. As he was leaving, the home's security guard called after him and asked whether the snack bar should be kept closed that night. Not comprehending the question, the director asked the guard what he meant. The guard, a gentle but bear-like cigar-chewing veteran of countless years at the home, said that it had been the policy to close the snack bar when the adjacent auditorium was used for such events as board or auxiliary meetings. Apparently the sight of the elderly in wheelchairs or using walkers was discomforting for some visitors. With obvious annoyance, the new director replied, "Open the snack bar. This is the residents' home, not ours. We are the intruders!"

My second example comes from my own experience as the CEO of health system that included as one of its central organizations a large nursing home. Shortly after I took the job, I met with the human-resources director to discuss the employee orientation. My interest in this subject was in large measure generated by my experiences doing research in Japan on hospital management (later published as a book). When I visited these institutions, I was astounded to learn that the typical orientation for new employees lasted several weeks and that the orientation was viewed as a major investment in the organization's future human capitol.

Further, the essence of the orientation was not the dispensing of technical knowledge but rather the sharing of philosophy and values. Two changes were instituted. First, we started scheduling the orientations once every three weeks. By doing this we always had a group of between fifteen and twenty-five people at the orientation sessions. And even though the people worked in different areas of the organization, the interdepartmental orientation was designed to and actually did result in a greater sense of total community that I believe benefited the residents.

Second, I insisted on giving the introductory "welcome lecture" every three weeks. This was not simply an ego trip but rather an attempt on my part to ensure that every employee understood our organization's history, values, and mission. I typically did this through a series of stories such as the accountant from our business office that observed a resident stranded in an outdoor patio area during a drizzle. Rather than ignore this person—after all the accountant was essentially a back-office person who had nothing to do with direct care—she approached the resident, asked if she could help, and then, in response to the resident's request, proceeded to push her into the vestibule of a nearby building. I would urge all our new staff to treat each and every one of our residents as honored family members—and as my friend in Massachusetts stated, remember that we are guests in their home.

While these examples illustrate the important role that management plays in the quality of life for nursing-home residents, the people with whom residents have the most direct and often most crucial contact are the members of the medical and nursing staffs.

## Medical-Staff Issues

Speak to anyone associated with nursing homes and they will tell you the same thing: "The residents are coming to us in a more debilitated state of health; they are older and need more intense care." From this should flow the conclusion that nursing homes have a significant medical staff, that is, a full- or part-time physician in attendance. Unfortunately, that is simply not the case.

While all nursing homes have physicians designated as medical directors, the reality is that most homes rarely have the benefit of a significant medical presence beyond the state-mandated minimum, which in some cases is as low as four hours per month. Typically, the medical director spends a few hours at the home each week, rapidly checking on a number of residents and spending even less time on the paperwork of medical care.

Each resident normally is required to have an attending physician in addition to the medical director whose job is primarily the administrative overview of the medical care at the home. In many cases the attending doctor also is the medical director, but residents retain the right to select their own physicians. So if it is mutually acceptable, the family physician may continue to serve as the nursing-home resident's attending physician.

Admission to nursing homes requires a physician's order, although sometimes a nurse practitioner can provide an admission order, which then is countersigned by a physician. An exceptionally well-run home will have a full-time medical director who is a gerontologist, meaning a physician whose clinical training as well as personal commitment is in the care of the elderly. Such a person is most likely to be knowledgeable about those clinical issues of geriatric care that have an impact on the daily life of a resident.

For example, there is considerable literature about medication problems with the elderly, a situation that a full-time medical director would no doubt be aware of and interested in evaluating. Some recent literature suggests that as many as half of the frail elderly who have been classified as totally incontinent can become continent through careful evaluation of their type of problem (e.g., urge, reflex, stress, overflow) and appropriate medical intervention. A physician working full-time with a group of people facing these problems on a daily basis is more likely to be attuned to resolving these issues than the occasionally visiting physician whose nursing-home rounds take five minutes per resident.

The full-time medical director, typically found in the not-for-profit or government homes, particularly facilities associated with medical schools and other training programs, is exactly as the term implies—full-time. One simple question will easily determine the status of any home's medical staffing: How many hours per week does the medical director spend at the home?

While the ideal model of the full-time medical director does indeed exist in many homes, there are several other options that homes can utilize in order to meet the need for a full-time, committed medical presence.

For example, in one home I visited, the twenty-hour-per-week medical director was provided with an office by the nursing home so that he could also conduct his private practice on the premises, thus ensuring his availability for emergencies, unusual problems, and casual consultations. A number of nursing homes have medical staffs that consist of several physicians whose total hours at the home exceed forty but who split their time between appointments at the home and teaching at a medical school.

Another home I visited employs a team of five physicians, each of whom takes responsibility for a different day of the week. Together they form a group practice for the home's residents. At a nursing home I visited in Missouri, six to eight senior medical students are at the home three times per week, augmenting the services of the part-time medical director and a full-time physician who is supported by a fellowship in gerontology from a local medical school.

A different option that also has merit is the combination of a part-time medical director and a full-time geriatric nurse practitioner who is a registered nurse with advanced training in assessing and treating the needs of the elderly. At these homes where such an arrangement has been developed, the geriatric nurse practitioners function under the supervision of a physician. Through the use of standard clinical protocols, the nurse practitioner is able to diagnose and treat a significant percentage of the primary-care needs of a nursing home's population.

## Nursing-Staff Issues

Central to the staffing of any long-term-care facility is nursing, which usually represents about 60 percent of the total employee complement. Three distinct groups of people provide the care delivered by the nursing department: registered nurses, licensed practical (or vocational) nurses, and aides.

Registered nurses (RNs) are those who have completed the requirements of a two-year community-college program, a three-year hospital-based nursing school (these are increasingly rare), or a four-year college-based nursing program. Following these programs, the graduate takes a state licensing exam and, if successful, is entitled to the designation RN, or registered nurse. In terms of practice, the RN has the greatest level of responsibility and authority for delivering care to a resident, which normally includes technical tasks such as giving medications and inserting and removing catheters, and supervisory and managerial functions, such as developing a nursing-treatment plan for a resident and ensuring that the plan is implemented.

At the next level are the licensed practical (or vocational) nurses (LPNs or LVNs), who, on average, account for between 15 and 20 percent of the total nursing staff. In functional terms, much of what the LPN does overlaps with the work of the RN, but the supervisory responsibility remains with the registered nurse. It is common to see LPNs taking vital signs (temperature, blood pressure, and respiration), administering medications, giving enemas, monitoring intravenous fluids, and in some cases supervising the nursing activities of a unit. The educational requirements for licensed practical or vocational nurses vary from state to state, but in general they include passing a state licensure exam subsequent to either graduation from a vocational high-school program or a one-year post-high-school training program.

The third and most populous group is the aides, who make up almost 70 percent of the nursing staff. Under current state and federal regulations, aides must receive between eighty and one hundred hours of training before certification. Aides are central to the delivery of a range of day-to-day care. For example, they are the people who bathe, dress, feed, and often transport the residents.

Of greatest importance to anyone looking for a nursing home is knowing how the regulations differentiate the required nursing times for the different levels of residents. The crucial measure used is "hours of nursing care per resident per day." In my travels, I have found that 90 percent of the nursing-home administrators or nursing directors could give me an instant answer to the question: "How many nursing hours per resident per day do you have?"

While each state sets minimum hours per resident per day by level of care, I do not believe that it is worth the energy to learn these numbers. However, for someone interested there are several ways to find out these minimums, but the easiest is to check with the administrator of a local nursing home. A second way is to call the state agency responsible for regulating nursing homes—the state department of health usually is a good place to start. A third, and interesting, way is to read the regulations: these usually are available on the Internet.

More important, in Chapter Ten I illustrate how simple it is to find the nursing statistics for any nursing home.

Why is this important? The extra half hour per day may not sound like much, but it does result in significant variations among facilities. For example, it could make the difference between a hectic or a relaxed environment or an enthusiastic or a burned-out staff. On a very practical level, it could spell the difference between having sufficient staff and having expecting families to provide regular assistance or employ nurses or sitters for the residents. On the other hand, the raw data are not enough: for example, employee turnover data would be invaluable. And nothing substitutes for a personal examination of the nursing home!

## Social-Services Issues

For many families, the first contact with a nursing home is through its social-services department. In promotional literature and residents' handbooks, this department frequently is defined as being responsible for the emotional and social needs of residents. Typically this means that the social-services staff usually provide information about the home and its services and the cost of care or help in applying for financial assistance. If a decision is made to apply to a home, social workers usually process the applications and may be involved in the testing and evaluation of the applicant. On the day of admission, someone from social services commonly is responsible for squiring a person through the transition from home to institution.

The social services staff also deal with any problems that arise during this period such as displeasure with a room or roommate or difficulties with the nursing home's schedule. Social services are required for nursing-home licensure, so states set educational requirements for social workers and stipulate the number of social-work hours a nursing home must offer. Typically, the smaller the home, the fewer the hours that must be offered.

Unfortunately there are some social-services people whose primary function appears to be recruiting financially secure private-pay residents. However, the vast majority of social workers whom I've encountered over the years were more interested in helping people than in filling beds. What this means is that the typical social worker is most likely to focus on educating the family about themselves, their needs, and the other resources that are available in the community to serve these needs. In practice a visit to a nursing-home social worker may result in a referral to a day-care center, assisted-living facility, or home health-care arrangements.

Following admission, the social worker frequently takes on the job of case manager, thus becoming an in-house liaison and ombudsman for the resident. This task involves resolving adjustment problems for both the resident and the family and responding to the needs of staff vis-à-vis a resident. For example, the nursing staff may want to have a resident or a resident's family clarify instructions concerning resuscitation of the resident in case of cardiac arrest.

## Physical Therapy, Occupational Therapy and Speech-Language Pathology Therapy Services

Therapeutic services are a category that nowadays means physical therapy, occupational therapy, and speech therapy. There are other important and useful therapies such as art therapy, music therapy, and even pet therapy, but unless for rehabilitation, these are typically not covered financially by Medicare and Medicaid. More about them in another section of this chapter!

Despite the importance of these therapies in maintaining and possibly restoring a person's health, the requirements imposed upon nursing homes for providing such services are limited. Unfortunately the limits are typically financial, but the nursing home is often required to "provide meaningful availability of restorative therapy services beyond restorative and maintenance nursing care."

The focus of physical therapy (PT) is the restoration of function, prevention of disability, and relief of pain. In response to a physician's order, the physical therapist develops a treatment plan as well as an evaluation that includes tests of muscle strength, gait analysis, body-part measurements, and a range of motion assessment. Treatments typically used by a physical-therapy department include whirlpools, ultrasound, hot packs, massage, parallel bars, and a variety of muscle-building devices, such as wall pulleys.

Occupational therapy (OT) is not job training but rather a significant component of the physical and emotional rehabilitation process. Occupational therapy concentrates on channeling the strength developed in physical therapy into daily living activities, such as homemaking skills and manual arts and crafts. Some occupational-therapy departments are involved in the design of an extraordinary variety of splints and other gadgets for assisting residents in regaining their independence.

The work of a speech and language therapist/pathologist (SLP) in a nursing home typically relates to various issues around the general category of apraxia in the form of either aphasia (a neurological issue) or dysarthria (which is related to muscle issues). Additionally, speech therapists are trained to work with residents on swallowing and feeding problems that are often significant issues in nursing homes.

These therapies are covered, to a limited extent, under Medicare. Every year the government sets an outpatient-therapy limit on these three therapies. For example, in 2017, physical therapy and speech therapy together had a cap of $1,980. Occupational therapy had a separate cap of $1,980. The unfortunately low caps often force families and administrators to make choices among the three vital therapies. A no-win situation all around! There are exceptions to the therapy caps, but in order for an exception to be made, an appeal must be made to Medicare with support from the patient's physical therapists. If the appeal is accepted, the thresholds are raised to $3,700 for the combined PT and SLT and $3,700 for the OT.

In general, state regulations require only that nursing homes have services available to residents and that the services be provided on the written orders of a physician. In practice, the concept of availability means that the facilities contract for services on an "as-needed" basis. In many homes, residents do not receive physical or occupational therapy on a regular schedule but only get the service for short-term needs from contractual physical or occupational therapists. Unfortunately, too many nursing homes have no dedicated area for such therapies, and the space utilized is often minimal and unpleasant.

## Activities and Recreational Services

Programs in art, music, and pet therapy found are in a small number of nursing homes. In most cases such programs fall under recreational activities that involve arts and crafts, music, or pets. Unfortunately neither Medicare nor Medicaid reimburses homes for these valuable therapies, so they only exist through volunteers, monetary donations, or, in some cases, school affiliations where students use the nursing home for field training.

Although all nursing homes have some type of activities program, here again there are great variations. Since most state and federal requirements are ambiguous and rather minimal, the differences are a function of a home's resources and its commitment to an activities program that is functionally related to the general therapy program.

A typical small home with 100 to 125 beds may have one or two full-time-activities staff members with training that varies from on-the-job experience to college degrees in recreational therapy. In terms of programs, virtually every nursing home has some of the following activities: arts and crafts, exercise, current-events discussions, games, religious services, and the old standby, bingo.

What distinguishes the run-of-the-mill place from the particularly interesting facility is the quality of the staff planning and organizing that goes into delivering a variety of timely offerings. For example, some homes give lip service to the residents' need for a library (and in some cases, the state requirement for one) merely by having a shelf full of discarded books and magazines recycled from a dentist's office. Others have fully stocked libraries with large print books, image intensifiers (magnifying glasses), and even books written in the mother tongues of the residents. Some offer residents trips outside the home to local attractions and eateries.

When my sister was a resident at the Jewish Home of Western Massachusetts, she loved trips away from the home for a day. Typically she and other residents would get on one of the home's handicapped accessible vans, and, with the assistance of staff and volunteers, they would have an outing for food and culture to a movie, museum, or tourist destination. These experiences became something very special for all the residents, and when my sister passed away, my brother and I established a fund at the home, the Roberta Bergman Fund, to ensure that these experiences continued.

One particularly interesting and impressive activity that exists in several homes is a work-activity center in which residents can spend several hours each day doing basic manual-labor jobs for pay. A pioneer in this activity is the Fairfield Jewish Home in Fairfield, Connecticut. As they note on their website, they arrange for residents who are interested to work "filling envelopes for mass mailing, packaging samples for marketing endeavors or putting labels on brochures." When I personally observed the workshop in action, I was impressed with the camaraderie of the group. It should also be noted that this was not volunteer work; the participants were paid on a piece-rate basis. While some might think of this as exploitative, I view it as another social activity that allows many a group of residents to feel productive and perhaps less isolated from their previous work world.

After eating thousands of meals in nursing homes and hospitals, I think it is fair to say that institutional food is not a substitute for "home cooking." Eating at a nursing home, even in the best of places, is problematic. The atmosphere of a small or large dining hall, the restrictions on diet, and the strictures on time grate on everyone. Indeed, if most of us were forced to eat all our meals in the same dining room of the same hotel 365 times a year, it also would become tiresome.

State and federal regulations on food service fit into the usual pattern of lofty objectives and ambiguous standards. A full-time dietitian or, as in most cases a consulting dietitian, has the responsibility of overseeing the nutritional content of meals as well as the diets of individual residents. Typically, a physician will order a special diet, such as salt free, and the dietitian reviews the diet and ensures that it is adequate in all other aspects (i.e., calorically and nutritionally). A food-service manager who may not be a dietitian runs the actual dietary operation. In an increasing number of cases, an outside company that contracts with the nursing home may provide the food-service functions. I've met with many of these vendors, and they are often quite good. However, whether the food is a product of in-house employees or an outside firm, the bottom line is how much money the home is willing to allocate to meals.

As in all other areas, there are significant differences in how meals are planned, prepared, and delivered. It is easy to envision, for example, looking forward to meals at the Seattle Keiro Home and a number of other facilities. At Keiro, for example, they offer two choices: Asian or Western. Over the course of the month, there is a rotation of the Asian meals that appeal to the different ethnic groups that populate their Seattle home such as the Japanese, Chinese, or Koreans.

There are even differences is the physical setting for dining in some homes. For example, some have separate, small dining rooms for each unit while others have larger dining rooms that resemble those found in restaurants. I've been in several homes where there is even a volunteer playing music on an organ or piano during mealtimes. On the other hand, there are a great many homes, particularly smaller ones, where meals, while nutritionally adequate, are delivered in "dining halls" that minutes before mealtimes were activity dayrooms. Frankly, to me these settings are reminiscent of army mess halls.

## Staffing the Remainder of the Organization

Dozens of other people are involved in the smooth operation of a good-quality nursing home. Laundry workers tend to the institution's laundry as well as the personal clothing of the residents; maintenance workers ensure the safety and mechanical functioning of the facility; the crucial housekeeping staff keep the place presentable and inoffensive; and business office people order supplies, pay bills, bill residents, and may act as personal bankers for residents.

All these people, along with the nurses, technicians, and others, act as the surrogate family for the residents. Their caring attitudes and behaviors make all the difference between a home that is supportive and rewarding and one that offers a horrible, distasteful, and degrading experience. As one tours a facility, they watch for signs that it is truly a caring place and not just a warehouse for the elderly!

## Hospital and Nursing-Home Relationships

While most of us wish to avoid hospitals, we recognize that at some point in life, there is a good chance we might spend a few days in one for some reason or another. In general, the visit is short and, thanks to the new systems of reimbursement, getting shorter. Our expectation is that the hospital experience will be "high tech, low touch"; that is, we will be poked and probed and treated with a full range of drugs and other therapies. We do not expect to develop long-term personal relationships with nurses, therapists, aides, housekeepers, food-service employees, or the administrator. The whole process, in fact, is expected to be impersonal, albeit friendly. In the end, we will have a repaired body and will return to our previous activities with a few modifications. Sort of a "Jiffy Lube" experience for the body.

Nursing homes are not hospitals. Quite the contrary! Because of the problems with which they deal and the nature of the clientele they serve, nursing homes tend to be "low tech, high touch" institutions. What a person did for himself or herself in the past is now done with the assistance of others. The nurses and aides help the elderly person get out of bed in the morning, go to the toilet, bathe, dress, eat, and take medications. The activities staff are around all day helping to stimulate the person's interest in and zest for life. The food-service personnel are cooking for the resident's health and enjoyment. The therapists are busily fighting the uphill battle against a deteriorating body (and perhaps mind). The social-services staff are trying to solve problems that range from financing the care to unpleasant roommates.

In fact, the nursing home is a new and frequently permanent place to live, and to a significant extent, the staff become an extended family. Staff members must take care of the intimate details of the resident's life, and in the end, they often can be seen sitting next to an elderly resident and holding a hand as life quietly slips away.

A number of years ago, the president of the board of directors of an excellent nursing home told me that because a nursing home is never "home," even in the best of situations, he did not think anyone should move into a nursing home unless it was *absolutely necessary*. Unfortunately, the concept of "absolutely necessary" is ambiguous. In the next chapter, I shall address this central question of the need for moving into a nursing home.

# CHAPTER 7

# The Need for a Nursing Home

*I couldn't take care of my apartment...I needed care.*
—Mrs. G. K., ninety-year-old nursing-home resident, Cleveland, Ohio

## Introduction

A while ago I stopped in to see Bill Goodman, an eighty-three-year-old man who was dying of cancer. The visit took place in the comfortable, one-bedroom Miami Beach condominium that he shared with Mildred, his seventy-eight-year-old spouse, who herself had health problems that included a recent heart attack and a stroke.

By all accounts, Bill Goodman was a perfect candidate for a nursing home, since he needed assistance in eating, bathing, dressing, using the toilet, and transferring from a bed to a chair or out of the chair and into a bed. However, despite his dependent state, he was able to stay home because of Mildred's support, the aid of a local hospice worker who came in twice a week to bathe him, and their fortunate economic status, which allowed them to have nursing assistance around the clock.

The Goodman case illustrates the important point that *need for nursing-home care* can be assessed objectively, but the fact that a need exists does not necessarily mean that someone has to move to a nursing home. Why and how did Bill avoid that? There are several reasons. First, like most people, he did not want to end his life in a nursing home. He wanted to spend as much of his time as possible in the familiar surroundings of his own home. Second, he had the support of Mildred, which translated into a willingness to radically alter her lifestyle to accommodate Bill's nursing needs. For example, not everyone would be so generous in allowing an unknown nurse's aide to move into his or her apartment and share his or her bedroom. Third, he had the financial resources to pay almost three full-time salaries for round-the-clock care.

The Goodmans were also fortunate to find competent and willing nursing assistants. Indeed, he was lucky to have located his caregivers just as they were completing another long-term nursing engagement. Sometimes, nursing assistance simply is not available, and the family is unable to provide the necessary care. For example, a few years ago, I received a letter from a colleague saying he was taking early retirement to spend more time with his wife, who was being institutionalized because of Alzheimer's disease. For years she had been taken care of at home by a rotating army of nurses, but finally he had exhausted all the non-institutional resources in the community, and the only remaining option was a nursing home.

Bill Goodman also was lucky to have a physician who was supportive of his desire to stay at home and willing to work to accommodate those needs. Finally, Bill and Mildred had the good fortune to live in a community that had such resources as the hospice to provide the essential backup to the family and other caregivers.

Not everyone who wishes to do so can avoid a nursing home, and in many instances a nursing home is a much better place to be than one's own home. In the following sections of this chapter, I shall examine the need for nursing-home care from the perspectives of residents, families, physicians, and bureaucrats.

## The Residents' Perspective

Traveling throughout the country, I've interviewed scores of elderly nursing-home residents. One of my routine questions has been "Why are you in a nursing home?" The most common answer, whether they were admitted from a hospital or from their private residence, was that they needed a level of care and supervision that only a nursing home was prepared to deliver. And frequently, some type of especially traumatic event, such as a death or a serious illness, precipitated admission to the nursing home. Here are some of their voices:

*I was in shock after my husband died. I was hospitalized, overmedicated, misdiagnosed as having Alzheimer's disease when it was the drugs that were confusing me.*—Mrs. I. M., seventy-seven years old

*I came here because I lost my family and my health.*—Mrs. E. W., eighty-three years old

*I took sick, my wife died, and my doctor recommended a nursing home.*—Mr. M. R., ninety-four years old

*I was in a bad depression after I lost a daughter. I wasn't eating.*—Mrs. S. W., ninety years old

Finally, many of these people were also logistically alone in the world. For example, they were people who never married or were now widows or widowers; they had no children or their children lived in distant communities or lived distant lives in local communities. Sometimes, the elderly simply did not want to disrupt the lives of their families, and they viewed a nursing home as the best available option:

*My husband was here for 1 1/2 years and I sort of got tired traveling every day to visit him, so I decided to join him in the home. After six months he passed away and I stayed on.*—Mrs. G. S., eighty-six years old

*When my wife passed away, I did not want to live with my children. I told them they have their own lives...why should I go mess them up.*—Mr. S. R., ninety-one years old

*I didn't want to go live with my children; it isn't a good idea. It's nice, but it is not a home of my own.*—Mr. M. R., ninety-six years old

*I surely wouldn't want to live in a home with my children; they have different ideas.*—Mrs. S. W., ninety years old

*I was living with my daughter and I did not like living with her.*—Mrs. S. D., eighty-four years old

*When I was ninety-one, my wife got very sick and moved into the nursing home. I came with her, and after she died I just stayed on.*—Mr. S., ninety-six years old

*My children are not interested in me.*—Mrs. G. F., eighty-seven years old

The testimony of these residents demonstrates that the concept of "need" for nursing-home care is multidimensional. For some, "need" means the home can satisfy some medical or clinical requirements, that is, the home functions as something akin to a subacute hospital. For others, and perhaps the majority of residents, the home is the apparent answer to complex psychological and social problems ranging from the inability to secure adequate household and personal-care assistance to familial estrangement. Sometimes it is simply a place where there are people with whom to interact all day. In the next section, I will examine "need" from the perspective of those who frequently are responsible for the decision and often carry heavy burdens of guilt about "putting" someone in a nursing home.

## The Family's Perspective

A family's perspective on the need for a nursing home frequently is of crucial importance to the final decision to institutionalize one of its members. Generally the family is dealing with one of three situations. In the first type of situation, the family member requires short-stay posthospital care for rehabilitation or skilled nursing. In this instance, the nursing home is functioning as a subacute hospital, and there is no intent to keep the patient more than a few weeks or months. The decision about institutionalizing such a person is fairly easy, since the only true but unlikely alternative is continued hospitalization.

A variation of this type of situation occurs when the family member is going to a nursing home after a hospitalization and there is no intention of having that person move back into a private residence. In a sense, the hospitalization presents the opportunity for a family to move an elderly person out of his or her home and essentially trap him or her in a nursing home when the patient is most vulnerable. In one family where I saw this occur, the nursing-home resident was bitter over the "ambush" until the day he died, and he took every opportunity to share his bitterness with his children.

This second type of situation as well as the third—where a person is moved directly from home to a nursing home—are actually quite analogous, because they bring up a variety of conflicting feelings for the family. These feelings range from a sense of perceived duty ("We have to do this in the best interests of the family or family member") to a strong sense of guilt and betrayal ("We should have been able to care for Mom"). On the following pages are four case studies that illustrate the issues and problems families face in dealing with the second and third types of situations.

Case 1: The Williams Family

I first met Mrs. Williams when she attended a lecture I presented to the residents of a large geriatric center. She was a well-dressed and attractive woman who I later learned was fifty-eight years old. She listened attentively, and because she was sitting next to a gray-haired woman with whom she had walked in, I assumed she was the woman's daughter.

As my presentation moved into the discussion phase, I decided to engage people by asking questions. So I began questioning some of the center's residents and then moved on to some guests; Mrs. Williams was among them. When I asked her a question, she smiled politely and said, "Hello." I then moved closer to her, asked the question again, and received the same response. After the lecture, I learned that she was a participant in the center's adult day-care program and was a victim of Alzheimer's disease.

About a year after I first met Mrs. Williams, she was admitted to a nursing home. Several months after that, I had a chance to talk with her sixty-one-year-old husband, who shared with me the situation that the family had faced:

*For the past three years, I have been running a nursing home in my house. I even had a hospital bed there and housekeeping and nursing staff twenty-four hours a day. I needed someone there to watch my wife all the time. Even though she looked well, she needed help with everything, including eating. And she could not communicate. Friends drifted away; if they only knew the importance of a kiss or touch.*

*I was never able to take care of everything. There was a parade of staff and I had to help schedule things among three people. Sometimes she needed an enema and the staff had trouble giving it to her; the aides were sometimes not qualified. I would come home from work at 4 o'clock and spend half an hour coaxing my wife to go to the toilet. I would just sit there and hold her hand. She also fell a few times and it was difficult to get her off the floor. Even though the day-care center was good, it wasn't enough. The whole family was being victimized by this disease. I wound up going to a psychiatrist. The final straw was I couldn't work, couldn't do my job. She had fallen down again and I had to get the ambulance over to pick her up. I wanted her to have both activity and dignity.*

*Putting her in the nursing home was an emotional defeat. But it is the best place for her. There are competent staff around throughout the day and I visit all the time. My kids and I are trying to get back to our lives now.*

Case 2: The Brown Family

In the space of fifteen months, the four children in the Brown family had to deal with the trauma of placing both their mother and their father in a nursing home. The case of the eighty-four-year-old Mr. Brown was in many ways the easier. During the eighteen months preceding his institutionalization in a skilled-nursing facility, he had suffered three strokes, and although his eighty-year-old wife had tried to care for him after the first two strokes, the burden from the third stroke was overwhelming. With some assistance from their physician, the family was able to place Mr. Brown in a facility about two miles from their home.

Shortly after Mr. Brown moved into the nursing home, the youngest of their children, Anita, a thirty-seven-year-old part-time commercial artist, gave up her apartment and moved home, ostensibly to care for her mother. As it turned out, Anita kept an irregular schedule, so there still was a need for someone to provide assistance to Mrs. Brown, who suffered from depression as well as Parkinson's disease.

The other three children, all of whom had families and lived between one and three hours away from their mother, became increasingly concerned about their mom's welfare. After a seemingly endless series of long-distance phone calls, it was suggested that Mrs. Brown get some part-time help. Anita vetoed the idea, stating that she had moved home "to take care of Mom."

Finally, three months before my meeting with Bernard Brown, the eldest son, a crisis occurred when Mrs. Brown wandered into the emergency room of the local hospital and was admitted for psychiatric observation. This hospitalization brought all the children together to confer. It was clear to all but Anita that something had to be done. What the family arranged was continued hospitalization in a private institution that would accept their mother for a short stay. While the results of this institutionalization were positive, there was still no long-term resolution of Mrs. Brown's situation.

The next step was to arrange for twenty-four-hour care by aides and housekeeping staff. This approach was satisfactory for approximately a month, but then the first group of staff left, and the family and their mother had to contend with a parade of unskilled employees.

After that, the family tried to get Mrs. Brown into the same facility as her husband, but unfortunately beds were not available. Finally, almost out of a sense of desperation, the children arranged for her to move into a not-for-profit home about fifteen miles from Bernard's house. They hoped that this facility would offer more social contact for Mrs. Brown as well as provide her with the kind of assistance she was not receiving at home.

In general, Mrs. Brown has prospered in her new environment, the family is relieved that she is being properly taken care of, and the three older children are pleased that they no longer have to deal with Anita about caring for their mother. Furthermore, preparations are now under way for transferring Mr. Brown, so he will be in the same home as Mrs. Brown.

### Case 3: The Lincoln Family

For thirteen years after Dr. John Lincoln retired from his professorship at the local university, he kept himself busy with his hobbies of stamp collecting, reading, and gardening, plus his duties as a volunteer at the local hospital. Toward the end of this period, arthritis in his hips and lower back began to make mobility increasingly difficult and painful.

At the urging of his oldest child, a pediatrician, Dr. Lincoln entered the hospital and had a bilateral hip replacement. After the operation, Dr. Lincoln worked very hard at the various prescribed exercises and physical therapy, but the deterioration of his back and the pain in the hip made for difficult days and nights.

His wife, Pat, who still worked twenty hours per week in a local insurance office, was a devoted helpmate during the entire period. She always got up early to get him set for the morning. She would help him get out of bed and make the trip to the toilet. After that, she would help him dress for the day and prepare his breakfast and lunch. In the afternoon and evening, she would again help him with his toileting and then prepare supper. Later she would help him get ready for bed. Twice a week, a home-health-care agency would send an aide to the home to help bathe Dr. Lincoln. Several times a week, the Lincoln children would stop by and provide some relief for their mother and company for their father. Once or twice a month, the family would help Dr. Lincoln into a wheelchair and take him for a ride or a trip to church. This pattern went on for over a year until Mrs. Lincoln's health gave out and she needed hospitalization for lower back pain—a condition doubtless related to the work this five-foot-tall woman undertook in maneuvering her two-hundred-pound husband around their home.

Mrs. Lincoln's hospitalization clarified the need for the family to enlist additional help. The oldest child was able to make arrangements for a person to go in forty hours a week to aid her parents with cooking, cleaning, and minor aide duties. However, a physical and psychological burden still rested on Mrs. Lincoln.

Finally, after another two months, the oldest child's husband called a family meeting and stated, "In everybody's best interest, Pop needs to be in a nursing home." Everyone agreed that he was right, but the next problem was deciding who was going to tell Dr. Lincoln. Mrs. Lincoln said time and again that she could not do it. It was not until months after Dr. Lincoln's institutionalization that she was able to acknowledge her acute sense of guilt and failure over his admission. She said she felt she had betrayed her husband. The youngest child, himself a thirty-year-old lawyer, was hesitant. The daughter stepped forward and volunteered. What she recalls most vividly about telling her father was that he already knew it was something that had to be done.

Of particular importance in this case study is that a son-in-law, not a daughter or son, was the person who stepped forward and stated clearly what was needed. I have seen that particular scenario play out many times, that is, neither the children nor the spouse want to say what is truly needed and it falls upon a daughter-in-law or son-in-law to utter the feared words that mom or dad needs a nursing home!

Case 4: The Stein Family

Until Max Stein was ninety-one years old, he was totally independent, including driving his own three-year old Chevy Impala. A World War II combat veteran, this tall, handsome man with a meticulously combed full crop of white hair was widowed when he was eighty-eight years old. Before a stroke disabled him, his days were filled with daily synagogue services in the morning followed by breakfast with his fellow congregants. The remainder of the day he used for shopping and volunteering once a week at the local hospital. He lived in a condo complex in Florida, and every Tuesday and Thursday morning, a housekeeper came to clean his condo and prepare meals of roast chicken or meat loaf that she wrapped and placed in the refrigerator for Max to heat up in the evenings.

Additionally, two evenings a week, he had a poker game with friends in the complex. Overall, according to Marty, his only child and a fifty-nine-year old unmarried man who lived in Boston, Max's cognitive and emotional state was great until the unexpected stroke and the hours that passed before the housekeeper found him on the floor and called the local emergency ambulance service

When I first met Marty, he told me that Max was in a rehabilitation facility where he was relearning some basic skills, including walking and most particularly talking. The time delay between the stroke and getting to an ER had resulted in a severe impairment of Max's speech. Marty consulted me because he was certain that his father could no longer live independently.

He also told me that he had no interest in retiring and moving to Florida to become his father's caregiver, nor was his dad interested in moving back to Boston. Finally, when Marty and I first met, there was the issue of finances because within a few weeks, Max's Medicare eligibility for rehabilitation services would be expiring.

Our conversation centered on the question: What next? I suggested he begin investigating the possibility of full-time help at home or an alternative facility that could provide the proper care for him. After consultations with Max's social worker and physician, Marty decided to find a nursing-home placement for him. I suggested several excellent homes—even some five-star facilities (more about the star system in another chapter). The decision made jointly by Max and Marty, especially Max, was to keep him in the same facility where he was getting rehabilitation services but move him to another section of the building for long-term-care residents.

In talking to Marty about this, he said, "There were several reasons for our decision. First, my father had become comfortable and felt safe in that home. Second, going back to the condo was simply not going to work. And third, I had to get back to my job and life in Boston and I felt he would be okay in that home." Was this the best decision? For them it worked! Would it have been my decision? Hard to say!

In these various cases, despite the availability of financial resources and the best efforts of a supportive family, it became necessary for someone to move into a nursing home. In each instance the move came after a period of at-home care that was marked by increasing emotional frustration and physical debilitation. The move into the nursing home, while traumatic, signaled the beginning of a new and more organized relationship within the family units.

## The Physician's Perspective

Nursing homes, like hospitals, require a physician's order for admission. Unlike the decision to admit to a hospital, where the physician usually is operating with some clear clinical protocols and a defined plan for the patient while in the hospital, the nursing-home decision is a murkier one that often puts the doctor in the middle of ambiguous family controversies. The distinction between these two decisions is an important one. A physician hospitalizing a patient normally has decided that the patient's condition requires the technological intensity or physical facilities of the hospital. Further, the general intent is to keep the person in the hospital for a relatively short span of time. In contrast to the hospital stay, the nursing-home stay might be expected to last for several years, and the facility itself is considerably less sophisticated technologically. In fact, most of what occurs in a nursing home could take place in a person's own home with the help of a dedicated family or paid aides and with certain modifications to the physical environment.

In light of the differences between hospitals and nursing homes, as well as the stigma attached to being in a nursing home, I found it unsurprising to learn from a number of doctors that when it comes to a nursing-home decision, they see themselves playing less of a clinical role and more of a psychosocial support role for the resident and the family. What this means for the practitioners is that they usually are cast in the part of the option raiser, permission giver, or facilitator.

As the option raiser, the physician is dealing with a person or family who either has not thought about the nursing home or has simply dismissed it without recognizing the value of that alternative. For example, one practitioner told me of the case of a widower with chronic heart disease who lived alone and received a great deal of assistance from both local social service agencies and a daughter who lived nearby with her family and also held a full-time job. At some point, it became obvious to both the physician and the daughter that this man needed twenty-four-hour supervision, but it wasn't until the doctor said, "Maybe we should consider a nursing home," that the topic became a legitimate subject for discussion.

In a closely related role, the physician is cast as the person who gives the family permission to do what any objective, disinterested observer would acknowledge has to be done. A frequent problem that the physician encounters when acting as the permission giver is that of handling the assertion, "Going into a nursing home is going to kill my mother." Two common responses are "You will be amazed at how easily she adjusts to the home" and

"It really is in her best interests." Not dealt with here is the often present and unarticulated sense of enormous guilt felt by families who place someone in a nursing home. In fact, statistically few people "die" from moving to a nursing home, most adjust to their new environments, and if the home is the only sensible option, then it needs to be exercised.

A third role the physician may play is that of facilitator. Here although the soon-to-be resident and the family have decided that a nursing home is the best option available, they do not know which of several homes would be best. The doctor is then placed in the position of suggesting several homes and perhaps telling the family what he or she thinks of each of them. As facilitators, physicians sometimes find themselves in the situation of trying to portray a person in a more attractive light (to both the family and a nursing home) in order to facilitate admission to a desirable home. One physician, who carefully medicated an obstreperous patient with tranquilizers prior to a nursing-home interview, described himself to me as a coconspirator with the family.

In sum, from a purely clinical perspective, virtually every physician with whom I spoke agreed that there are plenty of patients who receive skilled-nursing care at home, but once the support systems start to fall apart, or the demands become too much for the support systems, then a nursing home becomes the best alternative.

## The Bureaucratic Perspective

Before someone goes into a nursing home, at least one and perhaps several bureaucracies may have to be dealt with, including the nursing home's admissions staff and, if the resident is a Medicaid recipient, a representative from the Medicaid bureau. Basically, everyone involved in the admissions process is looking at the same issues: whether a person's needs are such that a nursing home is the right place and what level of care the person needs.

In general, these needs are measured by activity of daily living (ADL) scales, which examine six areas of possible dependency: (1) bathing; (2) dressing; (3) using the toilet independently; (4) transferring, that is, getting into and out of bed or a chair; (5) bowel and bladder control (continence); and (6) eating. There is also a secondary scale that addresses the needs of the elderly but usually is not applied to nursing-home needs because it focuses on skills involved in being independent and managing in a community. This scale, called the instrumental activities of daily living (IADL), has a number of components that evaluate the difficulty a person has with the routine tasks of daily living, such as shopping, doing laundry, taking medications, going for a walk, and cleaning up the house.

For the new resident who will pay privately, the process usually is fairly streamlined. In such cases, the agreement for institutionalization and level of care is made between the nursing home and the individual or his or her representative. But in many instances, being ready, willing, and able to pay does not guarantee admission, particularly in a situation where beds are not readily available. Also, in some states, regardless of how the bill will be paid, the state must approve the level of care placement—the rationale being that someday the resident could run out of private funds and the state would have to pick up the bill, so it wants to be sure the placement is correct from the start. Finally, under present federal legislation, all new admissions must be prescreened for mental illness and mental retardation. This program started in 1989 is known as the PASRR, that is, Preadmission Screening and Resident Review. This program requires a preadmission determination of the mental illness, mental retardation, or developmental disability status of a potential nursing-home resident. In a 2014 review of this preadmission screening program that was commissioned for the US government's Center for Medicare and Medicaid Services, it was found that in "most states PASRR under-identifies individuals with serious mental illness, and to a lesser extent, intellectual disability." This could lead to a lack of services for people suffering from these problems and potentially a disruptive environment for other residents when services are not available.

On a private-pay admission, it may also be necessary to demonstrate a *need* for care, which is likely to be determined by a member of the nursing home's social-service or admitting staff. In general, these people are looking for a new resident who needs the home's services but will not become an inordinate drain on its resources.

The determination of need for care will be made from data generated from several sources. One source will be a summary medical report provided by the prospective resident's physician. This report will ask for current diagnoses, past medical and surgical history, such other basic medical information as allergies and immunizations, and the recent report of a physician. Frequently the doctor will be asked to provide information about a person's family and social history and data about medications and diet.

A second source of information comes from the application form. These forms typically request information about the applicant's social and clinical background as well as financial resources. The third and perhaps more significant data source is that generated by the nursing home from an interview with the prospective resident and his or her family. This interview will probe the prospective resident's ability or lack of ability to handle the activities of daily living, most particularly, bathing, toileting, dressing, ambulating, eating, and transferring. Additionally, the interviewers place emphasis on the person's cognitive state, and some institutions even run the prospective resident through an evaluation. Finally, there is a subjective dimension, which does not ask whether the applicant needs the home but rather whether the applicant will *fit into* the home. The answer to that question is equally important; since no home wishes to burden itself with a disruptive resident (*or* family) for the *several* years that he or she is likely to be there.

The prospective resident who is a Medicaid recipient and is hospitalized may have a shortcut into the nursing home. If the doctor determines that the patient should be in a nursing home, the hospital's discharge planners and social workers usually will prepare the person for the nursing home and even go so far as to arrange the placement. When the hospital staff goes through this process of determining a person's need for care, it usually is merely countersigned by the Medicaid bureau, which has essentially delegated the determination of need to the hospital staff. *For* the prospective resident and his or her family, the *problem* with this is the pressure to accept the home the hospital has selected. Refusing to use that home *places* them at risk of having no nursing-home bed and potentially continuing in the hospital but being responsible for some portion of the bill.

The *last* possibility is that a person presently living outside of an institution now needs to be in a nursing home. In such a situation, the Medicaid bureau may send a field worker to the private home to determine the person's eligibility for care. Although there appears to be a scoring system to quantify the data, in practice the scoring system is not used, and it is the judgment of the field worker, typically a nurse, that results in a decision. If the applicant's physician agrees with the field worker's decision, the placement proceeds. In the case of disagreement, there is an appeals process.

In the most common situation, an individual is already eligible for Medicaid and his or her health condition has deteriorated to such a point that family members can no longer be the caregivers. Medicaid is called, a field worker is dispatched, and a determination is made within a week or so that the person is a skilled- or intermediate-care case. Once the level is determined, the individual is essentially certified and the family can proceed to look for a nursing home. Sometimes a family places the person in the home first and the determination comes later. Obviously, such an approach runs the risk of a denial, in which case, the family or the resident may be personally liable for the nursing-home bill.

When the Medicaid staff denies a nursing-home placement for someone, it usually is because some less expensive alternative, such as adult foster care, rest home, or home health care, is available. In some states when this occurs, the Medicaid branch will provide assistance to the recipient in finding proper alternative services.

## Conclusion

Despite various attempts to define the concept of need objectively, in the end it still remains an elusive idea and a subjective decision. The American health and social-service system is at times illogical, such as with the adult foster-care programs throughout the country that will pay unrelated parties daily or monthly fee (tax free) to care for the elderly in their home but will usually not give either a dime or a tax break to a family that provides the same care to one of its own. Since 2015 people have the ability to hire family members to care for them at home—but there are many hurdles to overcome under what is called the "self-directed long-term services and supports (LTSS) programs." The VA also has a similar program. Clearly, a fair percentage of persons in nursing homes could be cared for outside of those facilities if there were adequate support systems in terms of family, social, and health agencies. On the other hand, those people who are in the nursing homes are probably there because no other alternative was realistically possible.

# CHAPTER 8

# The Costs of Nursing Homes and Alternative Long-Term-Care Options

## Nursing Homes

Just like first-class travel on an airplane, private-pay accommodations are enormously expensive! Since 2002 the MetLife Mature Market Institute, a division of the Metropolitan Life Insurance Company, in association with LifePlans Inc., a consulting firm, has been doing surveys of long-term costs. Their report from November 2012 provides the following rather startling information: The average private room in a nursing home costs $248 per day or $90,520 per year while a semiprivate room for private payers averages $222 per day or $81,030 per year. Additionally, some nursing homes offer specialized units for Alzheimer's and dementia care, and the survey reports that the costs of rooms in such units is $261 per day for a private room ($95,265 annually) and $230 per day for a semiprivate room ($83,950 annually).

Of particular note is the variance of costs both across the country and across any given state. For example, the highest average cost for a private room is in Alaska with a figure of $687 per day ($250,755 per year). Within Alaska the low end of the range is $452 per day ($164,980 per year) to a high of $998 per day ($364,270 per year). At the other extreme is Louisiana with an average private rate of $157 per day ($57,305) and a state range for a private room from $132 per day ($48,180 per year) to $250 per day ($91,250 per year). Overall the lowest private rooms available in the country appear to be in the Dallas–Fort Worth area of Texas at the rate of $90 per day. Sounds like a regular bargain, but it still works out to $32,850 per year and with the average length of stay being two-and-a-half years someone needs to be prepared to spend in excess of $80,000 for a private room in the least expensive place in America!

Of course, just like hotel rooms, there is a huge difference between a $90 room and a $900 room. On the other hand, it is worth remembering that nursing homes are much like airplanes, that is, the first-class passengers may get a few more amenities but thanks to an enormous amount of oversight, the "first class" and "economy" residents of a nursing home essentially get the same quality of care.

So while Medicaid programs will essentially cover room, board, nursing services and all the related services such as activities, there are other items for which the resident, even those on Medicaid, will be responsible.

Finally, there are many additional costs associated with being in a nursing home that are most frequently spelled out in the admissions contract (see appendix) or by law in the case of residents who are being paid for by Medicaid. Some typical examples might be purchases of books or magazines, stationery or stamps, a visit to a hairdresser, or perhaps a meal outside of the nursing home with family members. The question then is how does a person who has depleted his or her finances or never had saved any money and is now in a nursing home under Medicaid has any funds for such personal needs. The answer is that every Medicaid recipient in a nursing home is entitled to a "Personal Needs Allowance" provided by his or her state program. The money can be managed by the residents themselves or through an account administered by the nursing home at no fee for the management. The amount that the resident receives monthly varies by state with an approximate range of $40.00 to over $100.00 per month. For example, Colorado provides residents $81.95 per month and Florida $105.00 per month.

When my sister was in a nursing home, she very much loved going on outings to local museums or restaurants. Sometimes the home, a truly outstanding place (the Jewish Nursing Home of Western Massachusetts in

Longmeadow, Massachusetts), would have one of its drivers and vans available and they would provide transportation gratis. The museum admissions and restaurant bill were my sister's responsibility. On a few occasions, the nursing-home van was unavailable and my sister had to rent a private vehicle and pay for both the vehicle and driver. Unfortunately, I do not have exact cost figures to offer with regard to the *extras*, but suffice it to say that a family or resident should not think that when a person enters a nursing home, all the expenses would be covered by a single payment.

While a nursing home is simply not an *all-inclusive* operation, there are significant variations between facilities about what is included. I've been to many homes that provide telephones, cable TV, snacks, laundry service, and even clothing. This is one of the areas for further investigation by a family before selecting a facility.

## Assisted-Living Communities

Perhaps it is best to understand *assisted living* as a crossover product, neither a skilled nursing home nor an independent-living community such as Century Village or Sun City, but something in between. The folks choosing to live in assisted living usually have some health deficit that requires some degree of *assistance*. Therefore, assisted-living facilities sometimes have characteristics of a nursing home, but they also look like independent-living apartments. For example, one project that I was involved with built two room suites. The bedrooms were merely bedrooms but were designed with call bells, skid-proof flooring, and good lighting. The bathrooms all had raised toilets, raised sinks, and showers with low lips, grab bars, and the ever-present call bells. The *living room* was small but functional and had a small refrigerator and microwave. It had been decided by our architects not to build more comprehensive kitchens because the expectation was that all meals would be provided to the residents in a central dining room. In addition to the dining room, there was a small exercise room, a therapeutic pool, a library/day room, and synagogue. It was a beautiful building and to this day is well maintained and well run and typically has a waiting list.

The MetLife survey provides 2012 cost data for assisted living. This data suggests that there are three base costs for assisted living based on the level of services. MetLife categorizes the costs based on whether just basic services are provided (five services or less), standard services are provided (six to nine services), or all-inclusive services are provided (ten or more). Since assisted living is not regulated as extensively as nursing homes, nor is the care as standardized as nursing homes, it is sometimes difficult to clarify what exactly are the basic services and the more extensive services of a particular facility. However, virtually every facility will offer meals, a twenty-four-hour system of security and monitoring, which can be formal or informal, some housekeeping and basic laundry, and often some transportation, exercise classes, and basic health services such as blood pressure monitoring. Only 4 percent of the communities surveyed were in the basic service category, and in 2012, they charged $2,751 per month ($33,012 annualized). The standard category representing 65 percent of the facilities had a monthly base charge of $3,486 ($41,832 annualized), and the all-inclusive operations representing 31 percent of the facilities had a monthly base cost of $3,789 ($45,468 annualized). More recently the Glenworth study of 2017 identifies the average cost of assisted-living facilities as $3,750 per month ($45,000 annualized).

The MetLife survey also provided data on average monthly cost for services that facilities may charge in addition to the base rate. Specifically, those homes that impose charges in addition to the base rate charge an average of $181 monthly for bathing assistance, $236 per month for providing a resident assistance in dressing, and $504 monthly for a resident who might need help with the other activities of daily living such as eating, toileting, or transferring. Finally, if a resident requires significant assistance with managing his or her medications, it would cost $347 per month. Doing the arithmetic—a standard average cost with all the add-ons—could cost in the neighborhood of $57,048 per year. And as is the case with nursing homes, there are variations from state to state and community to community.

A *New York Times* article on February 3, 2018, reported on the Government Accountability Office (GAO) study of assisted-living facilities. The GAO's finding was that the states and federal government were spending billions of dollars each year for over three hundred thousand Medicaid beneficiaries living in nursing homes with little to no oversight of quality. Indeed, the title of the GAO report says it all, "Improved Federal Oversight of Beneficiary Health and Welfare is Needed."

Finally, each state has many of its own rules and nomenclature. For example, in Texas, there are Type A, Type B, and Type C licensed assisted-living facilities. The Type A facilities are for residents who can basically evacuate themselves from the facility in case of emergency by following the instructions of staff. The Type B residents can't follow directions to evacuate and theoretically will have to be led, wheeled, or carried out. This distinction also means that Type A residents do not (according to statute) require "routine attendance during sleeping hours." On the other hand, Type B facility residents do "require staff attendance during nighttime sleeping hours, and require assistance transferring to and from a wheelchair." The Type C classification is for small four-bed facilities that basically meet minimum standards for adult foster care.

The Texas Administrative Code goes on to provide an overview of the needs of assisted-living residents and answer the question what are personal-care services for these residents.

## The Staying-Home Alternative

Staying in one's own home is neither cheap nor the best alternative unless a person has very few health issues, is not socially isolated, and has the resources to be at home. The MetLife survey found that a daily live-in home health aide would cost on average $251 per day or $91,615 per year. A live-in person who functioned as a companion and homemaker would be $4 less per day but still cost $90,155 per year. This cost is artificially low because it does not include the expenses associated with continued living at home such as rent, electricity, food, and the additional expenses associated with another person in the home. Also it should be noted that these arrangements whether with home health aides or homemaker—companions—are quite limited in terms of health/medical care. These aides may cook; clean the living quarters; help with bathing, toileting, and meals; or even drive someone around town. But here is an important caveat: one should not equate these aides to clinically trained personnel. Therefore, if there are medically complicated issues to be dealt with, it may be necessary to have a licensed nurse either on premises or supervising on a daily basis.

Where I live in Florida, these aides are omnipresent with their employers in condo developments, at the movies, stores, and supermarkets. Many of these employers hire the aides through agencies or word of mouth and pay between $60,000 and $100,000 per year plus the aforementioned living expenses. However, some folks manage to find unlicensed aides and companions as well as undocumented immigrants who will become live-ins for considerably less per year.

From a purely financial point of view, staying at home when a family member is not the caretaker is very expensive. As an illustration I have used the annuity estimator from a leading financial services company. Based on their estimates, an eighty-five-year-old woman who needed to spend $100,000 per year on an aide would have to invest, as a minimum, $800,000 in an annuity. With such an initial payment to the company of $800,000, there would be no payments from the annuity to beneficiaries after the death of the woman. If our hypothetical woman of eighty-five years age wishes to leave her beneficiaries some money, she could put $1.6 million into an annuity, which would guarantee twenty years of payment to either the woman or her beneficiaries.

## Adult Day Care

In the course of my professional life, I have been involved with several adult-care centers, and in general I believe they are an invaluable part of the spectrum of care for the elderly. Unfortunately with less than five thousand available nationwide, they aren't always readily available or accessible. The services these facilities provide typically include social, transportation, meals and snacks, and exercise, and oftentimes they can arrange some clinical services. A major limitation of many programs is that they operate five days per week and frequently between normal business hours with only about 10 percent of the facilities operating twenty-four hours a day.

In the lingo of the trade, there are three models of day-care centers. The least clinical is the social model (33 percent), the most intense clinically is called the medical health model (23 percent), and then there is a combined model (44 percent). None of these models is cheap! According to the Glenworth 2017 Annual Cost of Care Survey, the cost of the medical/health model center averages $70 per day ($350 per five-day week or an annualized cost of $18,200). The good news is that every state Medicaid programs will pay for all or part of a day-care program. However, for those elderly who are not Medicaid beneficiaries, the source of funds for such programs will be either self-pay or, in some instances, long-term-care insurance. One additional comment: regardless of payment source and the quality of the program, day care is exactly what the program is—day care! The responsibility for evening, weekend, and sometimes holiday care falls squarely on the shoulders of the family.

Finally, as with other stay-at-home options, the expense of continuing to live at home versus moving into a facility should be part of the calculation.

## The Pace Programs (Program of All-Inclusive Care for the Elderly)

When I wrote *Choosing a Nursing Home,* I devoted several pages of the book to "On Lok," a San Francisco–based innovative approach to provide health care to the elderly in the Chinatown area. The seeds and later implementation of On Lok came from a local dentist, Dr. William Gee, and a social worker, Marie-Louise Ansak. Together they built a demonstration project whereby hundreds of otherwise nursing-home-eligible elderly could continue to live in their homes but get a broad range of social and clinical services (including meals and transportation) on a daily basis from five-star adult-day-care service.

Years later On Lok has continued to be successful with many more programs and covering a broader group of communities. But what is of national importance is that this initially small innovative program in San Francisco became the impetus for the national PACE program whose mission is to essentially provide care to the elderly who are nursing-home eligible but provide that care at home and in day-care centers at a cost that is much less than providing it in a nursing-home building.

Today there are 123 PACE programs operating 233 PACE centers. These programs are in thirty-three states and serve forty thousand people. To see if there is one near you, go to the national PACE website, www.npaonline.org, and click on "Find a Pace Program in Your Neighborhood."

Finally some states have their own nursing-home diversion programs such as New York's "Nursing Homes without Walls" program, also known as the Lombardi Program, for Medicaid-eligible chronically ill and disabled. This program is for people who could qualify for nursing-home care but want to stay at home. In my judgment these and other programs are certainly worth exploring under the right circumstances, that is, someone else is at home who can provide support and oversight and the house itself is the organization to be safe for the patient.

## Design Options for Staying at Home

If there is a desire to stay at home, it is imperative that the house or apartment be modified so that it is maximally safe, accessible, and user friendly. For example, it may be necessary to install wheelchair ramps, grab bars for toilets and showers, skid-proof floor surfaces, emergency communication devices, good-quality lightings, stove alarms to prevent fires, motion-activated message players to remind people to take their keys or medications, or overflow shutoff systems for baths. There are literally hundreds of adaptive devices and home-modification possibilities available so that the elderly and disabled will be able to safely live in their own homes.

Among the resources available are state-funded assistive technology centers, for example, in Florida the program is called FAAST (Florida Alliance for Assistive Services and Technology). To search for the program in your own state, go to the website of the Association of Assistive Technology Act Programs (www.ataporg.org), and under the tab "About ATAP," scroll down and select "Find Your State Program." As a "test drive," I selected the Commonwealth of Massachusetts and learned that the MassMATCH program has regional centers throughout the state where consumers can "learn about, try out and borrow assistive technology." The organization also offers free used equipment and devices. On the day I checked their website, there were available bath benches, bed accessories, particularly rails, mechanical and manual slings, walkers, and wheelchairs. Particularly valuable were the photos and excellent descriptions of these free items.

Additionally, there are several industry trade associations that can provide useful information. One of them, the Assistive Technology Industry Association (ATIA), holds an annual conference in Orlando that brings together over one hundred exhibitors of adaptive equipment and technology. While the conference is primarily for professionals in the field of rehabilitation, it is also open to consumers.

One of the most expeditious ways to redevelop living space for the elderly may be to use a consultant with expertise in this area of work. One such person whom I worked with at the Miami Jewish Home and Hospital for the Aged is Beth Kofsky, a person with decades of experience and a certified environmental accessibility consultant and certified aging in place specialist. Her company's website provides a wealth of information about what may be possible in terms of home modification and products to make life better and safer for the elderly (www.housingandassistivetechnology.com).

Most important, the resources link on her website will help consumers locate similar specialists throughout the country. For example, through her "resources" link, I got to the National Association of Home Builders website (nahb.org) and on that site found "Find a Certified Aging in Place Specialist (CAPS)." Clicking on that I went to the next page where I clicked on the heading "Professionals with Home Building Designations." This took me to the following page to refine my results; in my case I was looking for a CAPS specialist, and I checked that box, and for my test case, I narrowed my search to Massachusetts, which had 176 specialists. In scrolling through the list, I found several builders in my community of interest with the CAP designation. It is definitely a good way to get started!

Sometimes a family member who is relatively handy can make the simplest of modifications such as checking to see that all the lightbulbs are working properly, removing or modifying obstructions to movements such as thresholds between rooms, or installing raised toilet seats with grab handles. More extensive projects such as installing a sturdy shower grab bar, changing out tubs or showers to become wheelchair accessible, or modifying door openings will clearly require a modicum of professional expertise.

## Medicare and Medicaid Payments

As noted in chapter 2, Medicare and Medicaid will pay for nursing-home care until a number of defined circumstances. Sometimes these circumstances are related to a person's health issues, hospitalization, or financial situation. In considering a nursing home placement, it is imperative to meet with the home's social workers and admission staff and clarify dollars and cents.

## Charges, Cost, and Quality

In nursing homes there is not always a perfect correlation among charges (what the resident is billed), cost of care, and quality. Indeed, many of the finest nursing homes that I have visited over the past two decades charged less than poorer-quality facilities. These excellent homes were typically of the not-for-profit variety, and they made up the difference between their charges and costs through extensive fund-raising and income from endowments. In those types of facilities, the residents were essentially subsidized by the home's fund-raising activities.

As far as direct resident charges are concerned, it is fortunate when the nursing home has a clear charge structure that can be compared easily with those of other homes. More often, though, it will be necessary first to identify all the services the resident is likely to require and then to ascertain the charges associated with those services. Only then it will be possible to compare rates. For example, many homes have an all-inclusive charge that may at first appear to be higher than rates charged by homes that essentially offer unbundled or à la carte rates. The true total can only be determined by adding all the expenses of the necessary ancillary services to their room and board rate.

While selection on the basis of price may be necessary in some instances, the issue of quality is of paramount importance for many people. Quality of care in nursing homes is a crucial and often confusing issue. For many families and residents, quality often is associated with the cleanliness or physical surroundings of the home.

Without minimizing the importance of a nice environment, it is also important to note that many nursing homes are truly selling the "sizzle and not steak." They often play on children's guilt about putting a parent in a nursing home and allowing these children to assuage their guilt by providing an environment with ersatz Chippendale furniture and a grand piano in a one-thousand-square-foot living room.

Of course, the reality is that residents cannot routinely use the living room for a host of reasons, including staff fear about soiled furniture from incontinent residents. A thoughtful purchaser of nursing-home care must look beyond these superficial aspects of quality. The next chapter begins the discussion of quality with an overview of the basic issues and an evaluation of some indicators and pseudo-indicators of quality care.

# CHAPTER 9

## Quality—The Elusive Component

*They need a lot of love.*
—K. G., A FIFTEEN-YEAR-OLD NURSING-HOME VOLUNTEER

### Introduction

A 2017 Google search of the bracketed term "Quality of Nursing Home Care in the United States" generates over eighteen million results. What this suggests to me is that while there is a great deal written about nursing-home quality, we still do not have the definitive word on this subject.

A number of years ago, I met with the health commissioner of a large industrial state, and one of the topics of our conversation was the quality of the several hundred nursing homes in his state. While neither of us had visited all the state's homes, we both had seen enough of them to agree that many presented problems in terms of quality of care. Our observations were very much in line with those presented by a number of congressional investigatory committees, the US General Accounting Office, and countless newspaper reporters aspiring to Pulitzer Prizes. Whether the information surfaced in newspaper exposés, congressional hearings, or carefully designed government research projects, the bottom line was always the same: a significant percentage of the nation's nursing homes deliver substandard care to their residents.

Since the commissioner and I both understood the reality, I asked him what he intended to do about improving the quality of the facilities in his state. The response I received was rather like a question I might pose to graduate students in a health-policy seminar: "How does the state simultaneously meet its various goals, which are apparently in conflict—that is, how does it improve the quality of care in nursing homes while holding or cutting reimbursement to these homes and also ensuring that the stock of nursing-home beds in the state does not shrink but rather expands?"

While this book is not about the public-policy problems in nursing-home regulation, the health commissioner's dilemma does have an impact on what a consumer can expect in terms of government supervision of the industry. Indeed, when the small army of state inspectors goes out to check the nursing homes, they are quite aware that while they can rough up the homes a bit, there are limits on how aggressively they can enforce regulations. And in most areas of the country, those limits exist because the states need the nursing homes more than the nursing homes need the states.

An individual consumer, however, simply does not have to worry about the quality of a state's five thousand beds; rather, he or she needs to be concerned about the quality of care given in only one nursing home. Since quality is one of the most crucial concerns of prospective residents and their families, this chapter provides a broad overview of the issues that are important for understanding quality. Specifically, it begins by defining quality within the context of the life of a nursing-home resident. Next, with a focus on food, a distinction is drawn between quality of care and quality of life. This chapter also discusses the serious and, unfortunately, bad news about quality, and a careful reading of this section will alert consumers to what experts look for as the benchmarks of quality. Finally, the chapter concludes with a discussion of the roles played by governmental agencies and voluntary organizations in monitoring and enhancing quality of care.

## Defining Quality

According to the many nursing-home residents whom I interviewed during my travels, good indicators of quality are cleanliness of the home, friendliness and attentiveness of the staff, adequacy and tastiness of the food, and freedom from urine odors. In many ways, their concepts are accurate manifestations of what researchers have also concluded as the necessary ingredients of a good quality home, including adequate staffing and attention to the individual needs of each resident.

Dictionary definitions of quality usually only provide us with abstract synonyms such as "excellence," "first rate," or "superior." Back in 1986, the Washington, DC–based Institute of Medicine issued a seminal report entitled *Improving the Quality of Care in Nursing Homes*. While this report never explicitly defined quality, it did provide important conceptual assistance by identifying what it considered to be the three major characteristics of an excellent nursing-home program:

1. A competently conducted, comprehensive assessment of each resident
2. Development of a treatment plan that integrates the contributions of all the relevant nursing-home staff, based on assessment findings
3. Properly coordinated, competent, and conscientious execution of all aspects of the treatment plan

In order to qualify on all three of the attributes set up by the Institute of Medicine, a home would have to be staffed with well-qualified practitioners, it would need to create a work environment in which people were well motivated, and it would need to provide the physical and managerial resources to effect the program.

Another approach was offered in a text authored by V. Tellis-Nayak titled *Nursing Home Exemplars of Quality*. Here three people—one university-based, one from the Illinois state welfare department, and a third from a provider organization—teamed up for a research project on high-quality nursing homes in the state of Illinois. Their search for what they characterized as the unsung heroes of a frequently maligned industry yielded eight nursing homes but did not really move us closer to a definition of quality of care. However, the examples cited by the authors reflected adequate resources, a commitment to something more than profits, interested and active leadership and management, and caring staffs.

Perhaps most interesting is the authors' final observation that while the "run-of-the-mill" nursing homes offer poor quality care, a number of other homes, acting under the same fiscal and regulatory constraints, offer quality care. This excellence, they suggest, "begins with a basic commitment to quality. As we have shown, in every first-rate home commitment goes hand-in-hand with a philosophy that sets the tone and defines the priorities. These homes then put together a cohesive management team that embodies that commitment, and single mindedly translates it into the daily routine of nursing home life."

## Distinguishing Quality of Care from Quality of Life

Food service is a good way of illustrating the difference between quality of care and quality of life in a nursing home. As is probably obvious, nursing-home residents are in many senses prisoners of the kitchen and the institution. Usually they are not in good enough shape to go out, and even if they are, there may be no easily accessible restaurant. Indeed, considering the scores of places I visited, precious few were located in a neighborhood where a resident could even stroll down to a corner grocery for a snack.

From a quality-of-care perspective, the first issue for concern is "Has the new nursing-home resident's diet been properly selected, based on an adequate evaluation by a physician or geriatric nurse practitioner and a dietitian?" A related quality-of-care issue is whether there is periodic follow-up on the nutritional status of the resident; that is, once a diet has been established, is the resident reevaluated at periodic intervals to ascertain how he or she is doing with it? For example, the diet of a resident who has diabetes or high blood pressure should be monitored and perhaps modified as the resident's health status changes.

A second quality-of-care question is "Is the food being served in terms of adequate nutritional value?" For example, is the resident receiving a sufficient amount of calories, and do those calories come from the appropriate food groups?

Other quality-of-care issues exist behind the scenes in the kitchen and storage rooms. For example, the quality of care can be undermined by poor sanitation in the kitchen or by food-service employees whose carelessness about personal hygiene transmits diseases to the residents.

However, all these and many other quality-of-care issues must stand in contrast to the quality-of-life issues that revolve around food. The nursing home interested in quality of life as well as quality of care recognizes the importance of food in the life of a resident. Such a home, while acknowledging the ever-present limits of institutional cooking and therapeutic diets, also recognizes that mealtimes for residents are as important for socializing as for eating. Such a home therefore approaches food as something more than merely fuel for the body. A few illustrations demonstrate how a nursing home can use food to enhance the quality of life for its residents.

When I first visited the Keiro Northwest Home in Seattle some years ago, I observed that residents of Japanese descent found Japanese foods on the menu at least once a day, and many traditional Japanese condiments are served with the western dishes. For example, while the usual breakfast might include toast, eggs, or cereal, several times a week breakfast at Keiro consists of miso soup, rice, toasted seaweed, or Japanese pickled plums. Lunches range from the western macaroni-and-cheese or meat loaf to fish teriyaki and various tofu dishes. Dinners tended to be mostly Japanese beef dishes or sushi. Nowadays, there is a rotation of Asian food choices as a way of accommodating the tastes of the non–Japanese Asian residents.

Encouraging family and friends to share a meal with residents is an easy and common policy in many homes. Several homes that I have visited have particularly nice dining rooms that residents and their families can use for special occasions.

A dignified and pleasant place to eat meals is another positive quality-of-life factor. As noted earlier I have visited many nursing homes where the main dining room is decorated like a room in a private country club or in a fine hotel, with wood paneling, wall sconces, and chandeliers. Waiters take orders from a selective menu and waitresses, check in the kitchen for dietary appropriateness, and then deliver to the table. I have also seen facilities where the head chef, in his or her full uniform of double-breasted white coat, checkered pants, and traditional mushroom-shaped tall white hat, keeps walking through the dining room and chatting up the "guests." Cookouts, ice-cream parties, theme parties, and special-occasion dinners, such as on Easter, Thanksgiving, Christmas, or religious occasions such as the Passover Seder, are very important for a nursing-home resident's well-being. If nothing else, they break up the monotony of eating 1,095 meals per year in the same place.

In trying to sort out what a visitor sees on an inspection tour, it is important to remember that we must look at the issues of both quality of care and quality of life. A glitzy dining room and no attention to a resident's dietary needs will be more damaging than a good, sound nutritional program and a modest dining room. The ideal is somewhere in between.

Finally, a cautionary tale. In one nursing home that I investigated, a resident's daughter complained to the management that she felt as if the home's inattentiveness to her father had resulted in the man's leg being amputated because of leg ulcers (secondary to diabetes) that developed in the nursing home. When I interviewed the nursing home's administrator and director of nursing about this situation, they basically stonewalled me and declared that the man had been receiving outstanding care and the daughter was merely a chronic complainer. I acquired the man's medical records and made an astounding discovery. According the nursing notes for the several months prior to his surgery, he was fully consuming his special diet every day yet he was losing weight every week. Despite this paradoxical and dangerous situation, no one requested a medical or dietary consultation—they just made their notes and allowed this man to deteriorate. Obviously an example of poor quality!

## The Bad News about Quality

In 1974, Mary Adelaide Mendelson wrote a superb exposé of the American nursing-home industry appropriately titled *Tender Loving Greed*. The research for her book involved studying the specific nursing-home problems of Cleveland, Ohio, as well as visiting some two hundred nursing homes throughout the country. Mendelson's pessimistic conclusion: "All over the country, nursing homes are similar, and similarly bad. Excellent homes are rare, and most of those that are considered good are good only by comparison to the majority that are worse." Indeed, of the two hundred homes she visited, Mendelson rated only one as a good home. What apparently impressed her about that home was the honesty of the staff in admitting their shortcomings and attempting to rectify problems.

A few years later, in 1977, *Too Old, Too Sick, Too Bad* was published. Jointly written by former US senator Frank Moss and Val Halamandaris, a staff member of the Senate Special Committee on Aging, this volume synthesized thirty congressional hearings held between 1969 and 1976 on abuses in the nursing-home industry. As a catalog of nursing-home horrors, this book takes the prize. Using the thousands of pages of testimony Congress received, the authors present a vivid picture of resident abuse, disgusting and unsafe homes, and profiteering owners. At one point they note "over 50 percent of the nursing homes are substandard."

While Moss and Halamandaris's estimate of 50 percent was based on their analysis of testimony to their committee, other estimates based on empirical research have also been offered. For example, in 1987 the US General Accounting Office (GAO) issued a report to Congress based on an analysis of Medicaid and Medicare inspections over a four-year period. The first goal of the project was to determine the extent to which nursing homes repeatedly did not comply with federal and state regulations that might affect patient health and safety. A second goal, formulated by analyzing data from five states, was to "evaluate the adequacy of federal and state enforcement actions to correct reported deficiencies."

Based on its review of national data, the GAO reached a conclusion that was not very different from that of Moss and Halamandaris:

*Forty-one percent of skilled nursing facilities and 34 percent of intermediate care facilities nationwide were out of compliance during three consecutive inspections with one or more of the 126 skilled or 72 intermediate care facility requirements considered by experts to be most likely to affect patient health and safety.*

Of greater concern, though, is what the GAO learned from its in-depth analysis of the inspection records of twenty-six problem-ridden nursing homes in Arkansas, California, Connecticut, Kansas, and Wisconsin.

Twenty-six nursing homes were selected primarily on the basis of multiple repeat deficiencies. Among the most frequently cited deficiencies were inadequate nursing services, poorly maintained and dirty interior surfaces such as walls and floors, malfunctioning or broken plumbing, uncontrolled odors, improper use of physical restraints, and improper diets.

The report goes on to note that despite numerous deficiencies, most of the homes were recertified, and two of the three that in fact were decertified—that is, were no longer eligible for Medicaid or Medicare funding—were readmitted to those funding programs within seventy-six days. Indeed, the GAO noted:

> *Facilities with deficiencies that do not seriously threaten residents' health and safety have continued participation in the programs for long periods without maintaining compliance with requirements. For example, a Kansas nursing home was cited in three consecutive inspections for having unqualified personnel insert or withdraw tubes used to administer drugs or provide nourishment, storing foods improperly, and failing to control facility odors, and in two inspections for failing to keep the building interior clean and well maintained. The nursing home received no penalty for the repeat deficiencies because termination was the only sanction authorized under Medicare and Medicaid.*

In December 1988, the US Department of Health and Human Services (HHS) threw another ingredient into the quality-of-care pot by releasing a seventy-five-volume state-by-state guide to nursing homes. With much fanfare, the departmental spokespersons explained that within these volumes, consumers could find three-page summaries of the annual federal survey reports on each home. These reports, it was explained, rated each of fifteen thousand nursing homes on thirty-two separate health, safety, and care standards. Overall, the federal report painted a bleak picture of nursing homes: 29 percent of the skilled-nursing homes did not administer drugs according to the written orders of attending physicians, 11 percent of the nursing homes failed to meet basic housekeeping standards, 43 percent failed the standards for storing and preparing food under sanitary conditions, approximately 25 percent did not use proper isolation techniques to prevent the spread of infectious diseases, almost 30 percent were cited for failing to maintain the standard of personal cleanliness of residents, and another 25 percent were cited for not properly caring for the skin of residents.

The response to the HHS report was predictable. The nursing-home industry chided the government for releasing confusing and outdated information; academics said that the fact that the nursing homes were decertified—that is, were no longer eligible for Medicaid or Medicare funding—was irrelevant since most were readmitted to those funding programs within seventy-six days.

Does anything change? At the end of 2015, the GAO issued another report on nursing- home quality where it examined four sets of data and concluded "nursing home quality show mixed results." Specifically it found that average number of serious deficiencies per nursing home surveyed declined, and staffing levels and clinical quality measures showed a slight improvement. On the other hand, consumer complaints had increased.

## Indicators and Pseudo-Indicators of Quality

### Indicator 1: Licensure of the Nursing Home

Periodically nursing homes are the subject of scandals, exposés, government reports, political statements, and tragedies. In 2007 during Hurricane Katrina, national attention was focused on nursing home in St. Francisville, Louisiana, where thirty-five elderly people lost their lives. In 2017, it was the tragedy that occurred in the Hollywood, Florida, nursing home where fourteen people died. All these negative stories and reports make it appear that there are simply *no* adequate nursing homes. *This is not the case*: there are numerous excellent homes with first-rate staff, programs, and facilities. The challenge is first to understand what the indicators of quality are and then to begin an investigation in pursuit of *one bed in the right home*.

Licensure does tell you that a home is bound by a range of rules and regulations with mandatory standards in such areas as sanitation, health, safety, and (as noted in chapter 1) staffing. What licensure does not indicate is whether the facility is in violation of any of the standards and what the nursing home is doing to correct the violations. Further, since licensure enforcement tends to be a problem in many states, it is important not to stop at this most basic of indicators.

## Indicator 2: Gold Stars, Gold Seals, and Medals

Some state governments, such as Kentucky and Texas, use to give out gold stars to their perceived best nursing homes. Most of these programs have been abandoned now that the federal government has its star system. Nevertheless states such as Florida have their own substitute programs such as the Gold Seal Awards. These programs likely operate with the idea that they can induce nursing homes to behave in a more responsible manner if they provide the homes with incentives to behave in the "right" way.

To accurately evaluate the importance of these special designations, it is necessary to contact the agency issuing the awards and find out what the standards are for the various designations, how those standards are evaluated, and, finally, how many facilities in the state meet those standards. For example, in Florida in order to get an award it is necessary to apply, provide a considerable amount of evidence of why you should be selected including data on financial soundness and stability, and be available for a presentation to the Governor's Panel in Excellence in Long-Term Care. While I suspect that most facilities that receive such an award are quite deserving of the honor, I also think that other deserving organizations have neither the time nor the resources to apply for the Gold Seal.

In 1996, the American Health Care Association, a membership organization composed primarily of for-profit nursing homes, developed an annual quality award program. There are three medal levels: bronze, silver, and gold. For example, at the bronze level, an organization must merely make a commitment to quality. The other medal levels require more intense scrutiny. While I applaud any activity that enhances quality, this data should be utilized along with the government's star ratings that I will discuss in the next chapter.

In the world of quality analysis, a common paradigm is to think about quality as a three-legged stool: structure, process, and outcome. The medal system tends to focus more on the measurable dimensions of structure and process. Is it valuable? Definitely, but it is not a surrogate for careful additional investigation of a home!

## Indicator 3: Licensure of Administrator

This is one of the most meaningless of indicators. For reasons that are not entirely clear to me, numerous pamphlets and other nursing-home guidebooks suggest that one indicator of quality is the licensure status of the nursing-home administrator. The reality is that for a facility to operate in most states and to be certified for Medicaid or Medicare, the administrator must be licensed.

Perhaps of greater importance is the relative ease of passing the licensure examination to become a nursing-home administrator. Frankly, it is not the equivalent of passing a state bar exam, a CPA exam, or the multiday, multistep US Medical Licensing Examination. Once an administrator is licensed in one state, it is quite simple to obtain reciprocity in other states as well as to renew the license by attending continuing-education courses.

Also, since the owners of private nursing homes, or the boards of not-for-profit homes, do not have to be licensed unless they actually function as the home's administrator, it is likely that the person who is the licensed administrator, particularly in a home operated as a for-profit corporation, may not have the major say in the policy and management of the home. Rather, as I have witnessed during my days as a hearing officer for as well as a member of the Board of Examiners of Nursing Home Administrators in New York State, the person pulling the strings maybe an unlicensed owner who is not involved in the day-to-day operations of the home.

## Indicator 4: Medicare and Medicaid Certification

Not every nursing home in the country is certified by Medicare or Medicaid. The decision of these homes not to be certified by these programs usually is based on economics—that is, the homes are interested primarily in catering to a totally private-pay clientele, and their market position allows them to do so without the constraints that governmental certification would impose upon them.

To be certified for Medicare and Medicaid, the nursing home must go through annual state inspections and meet hundreds of requirements that are focused on the structure of the home and the procedures it follows. The assumption behind the certification system is that a home will be better for its residents if it is properly structured—for example, if it has the correct policies and staffing in place and it follows the correct procedures, such as for administering drugs to residents. Looking back at what happened during Hurricanes Katrina and Irma, one must also wonder about the scope of these regulations and how well they are implemented!

## Indicator 5: Organizational Memberships

Nursing homes, like most other business enterprises, frequently belong to a number of trade associations. Since membership in these organizations normally requires nothing more than payment of dues or perhaps endorsement of a vague set of ethical precepts, such membership is essentially meaningless in terms of being a guarantee of quality.

The fact that a nursing home is a member of the Chamber of Commerce, the Better Business Bureau, the United Way, the American Health Care Association (the trade organization of for-profit homes), or the American Association of Homes for Aging (the trade association of the not-for-profit nursing homes) should be of no consequence in the decision to select or reject a particular home. This does not suggest that such organizations do not provide a valuable function but rather that membership in them simply is not an indicator of quality.

## Indicator 6: Accreditation Status

Accreditation is a horse of a slightly different color since it is handled by the Joint Commission on Accreditation of Healthcare Organizations, the same organization that accredits hospitals. For nursing homes, accreditation is a voluntary process that involves a home's being inspected during a several-day period by a team of outside experts who compare the activities within the home to a set of externally developed standards.

As with the licensure process and the medals, the reviewers are looking primarily at the structure of the organization and the processes within it. Presently, accreditation of nursing homes tends to answer the question, "Can this organization provide quality health care?" What the accreditation process does *not* tell us is the answer to a different question: "Does this organization provide quality health care?"

While the commission should be applauded for its diligent work on shifting accreditation from a process-and-structure orientation to one that focuses more on quality of care and outcomes, the reality is that accreditation status currently is of limited value to the consumer. Some nursing-home administrators I interviewed indicated that it was not particularly difficult to become accredited and that they simply used accreditation for marketing purposes. Even if these comments are accepted at face value, accreditation nonetheless indicates that a home is voluntarily opening itself to review by outsiders—and that, in and of itself, is positive.

In sum, if a home is accredited, it is a plus factor but not necessarily the ultimate statement of excellence. On the other hand, a home should not be viewed as unacceptable merely because it is *not* accredited by the commission. Indeed, some of the best homes I have seen are not accredited.

## Indicator 7: Teaching Affiliations

Nursing-home teaching affiliations come in a variety of guises. The premier affiliations are those with medical schools and teaching hospitals. When I was researching *Choosing a Nursing Home*, I had the privilege of interviewing T. Franklin Williams, MD, one of the founders of the field of geriatrics. At the time I met him, he was director of the National Institute of Aging, a division of the National Institute of Health. As his 2011 obituary points out, he also served for fifteen years as professor of medicine at the University of Rochester and director of Monroe Community Hospital, which was truly a misnomer since in reality it was a large skilled-nursing home that had developed a reputation for excellence.

This excellence was doubtless due to the leadership of Dr. Williams and the home's affiliation with the University of Rochester, which managed the facility and based some of its medical-school faculty there. The result of such an affiliation is the traditional commitment of a medical school or teaching hospital to quality, plus increased visibility and the scrutiny of the facility by a professional public vitally concerned with quality. Dr. Williams pointed out to me that the teaching nursing home has three advantages for its residents: (1) the resident is likely to find a higher quality of professional staffing because of the affiliation, (2) the presence of students who "are eager and often have the time and availability to care" is a big bonus, and (3) the teaching milieu often results in higher standards for the nursing home's management.

During my years at the Miami Jewish Home, we had a relationship (still ongoing) with the University of Miami Miller School of Medicine, Jackson Health System, and the Veterans Affairs Medical Center in Miami. The UCLA Geriatric Fellowship is operated jointly with the Greater Los Angeles VA, and it too uses local nursing homes for some of its training. In another example the medical school at Emory offers a clinical fellowship in geriatrics that also uses a VA nursing home as well as several homes that are part of the Wesley Woods system. A final outstanding example is Hebrew SeniorLife based in the Boston area and affiliated with Harvard Medical School. Over the years

Hebrew SeniorLife and its various components have trained numerous physicians and also made major contributions through its various research entities such as the Institute for Aging Research. Furthermore, perhaps because of its teaching affiliations, it has been a leader in organizational innovations such as their Lifecare community at Orchard Cove. Regardless of the specifics of any affiliation between a nursing home and a medical school or teaching hospital, it appears that any such arrangement has a positive outcome for the quality of the services in the home.

A number of nursing homes also have teaching affiliations with programs for training nurses, aides, technicians, therapists, social workers, and administrators. Generally, these programs reflect positively on the home, but they should not be considered as major statements of a commitment to quality. The reason for this is simple: most of the teaching programs focus on the educational experience of the student and simply do not delve into the job of evaluating or influencing the quality of care in an institution.

## Some Final Issues on Quality

### Chain Homes, Hospital-Owned Facilities, Nonprofit Facilities, and Mom and Pop Homes

An interesting issue is whether a person is better off in a facility that is owned by a national chain, an individual owner, a hospital, or perhaps some nonprofit corporation. I wish there were an easy answer to this question! I think the only honest answer is it all depends on the individual facility, its staffing, and its management.

For twenty-one years, I was on the board of directors of a chain of nursing homes. Also during several of those years, I served on the boards of two nonprofit nursing homes as well as being the CEO of a major geriatric center that included a five-hundred-bed nursing home. As noted earlier I have visited many mom and pop facilities as well as hospital-owned nursing homes.

And based on those experiences, I believe the best answer is that the only way to know which facility is the correct one for a family member is to learn as much as possible about the place and visit it several times. Frankly, as noted elsewhere in this book, put at least as much effort into shopping for a nursing-home placement as you would in buying a car!

## Special-Focus Facilities and Facilities under Corporate Integrity Agreements (CIAs)

Occasionally the consumer will learn that the nursing home that they are considering is a "special-focus facility" or alternatively is under a "corporate integrity agreement." Essentially what this means is that the Office of the Inspector General of the US Department of Health and Human Services has decided that the facility needs additional oversight from the government for a period of time, often several years. The reason for this oversight is typically related to the quality of care and frequently is a matter of dispute between the government and the owners.

However, the real and immediate issue for the consumer is whether such a facility should be avoided. In my opinion the answer is simply that such facilities should *not necessarily* be avoided. In fact, because of the heightened government scrutiny, it is quite possible that the quality a resident receives in such a facility will be good. These may be the best bargain nursing homes, but one must be certain that such homes have made the commitment to change for the better. If such a situation exists, the educated consumer should request a copy of the CIA or examine the document on the Internet by simply searching for the name of the nursing home in question and "corporate integrity agreement." Such agreements are a matter of public record. After reading the CIA, and perhaps seeking additional advice from an attorney, the consumer will be fully informed and better able to make an informed decision about the nursing home in question.

## Conclusion

Finding a nursing home that offers quality care is not an easy task. The nursing homes themselves frequently sell style and not substance; this does not make the task of choosing a nursing home any easier. And as various studies and reports demonstrate, the government does not make the task any easier, either.

In the end, it is the consumer who must separate the wheat from the chaff. To do this effectively requires research, knowledge, and effort. This process begins in the next chapter with an example of the three-page summary of a nursing home's evaluation, which is available for homes throughout the country.

# CHAPTER 10

## Being an Educated Consumer—Finding the Right Home

*Caveat Emptor (Let the Buyer Beware)*

Some interesting analogies exist between the processes of selecting a nursing home, a college, a job, and perhaps a car. For example, the governing principle in my family for college selection when I was graduating from high school was that we could go anywhere that we received a scholarship or, alternatively, anywhere that the New York City transit system could take us on a token (they didn't have swipe cards in those days) and a transfer. This simple approach limited choices and made the decision relatively easy.

Today it appears that, despite the enormous cost of a college education, tens of thousands of high-school students and their families are taking a broader and more aggressive approach to finding the right college. They start identifying possibilities by speaking with friends, acquaintances, school-based counselors, and even high-priced consultants. Next the student and the family peruse college websites, as well as the plethora of material colleges mail to prospective applicants. While both star athletes and star scholars can expect everything from letters to visits from recruiters and alumni to invitations for trips to distant campuses, in the more typical case, a parent winds up traveling with a high-school junior or senior from city to city, campus to campus, and admissions office to admissions office. Eventually, they will have visited a number of campuses; taken tours; talked to students, administrators, and perhaps faculty; and formed impressions about the colleges. Finally, they select a small number of schools for application, and from those schools that accept the student, they choose one for matriculation.

The processes of finding the right job and the right community are equally time-consuming. Someone searching for a new position usually has to pursue countless leads, submit résumés to scores of companies, and interview at dozens of firms before finding the right one. Then the second part of the equation comes into play: Is it the right community? People frequently select or reject jobs for such factors as the cost of living in a community, housing, taxes, and the quality of the elementary or secondary education schools. In my own case, I turned down one excellent job offer because the commute (after I tested it on two occasions) would have been horrendous and another because, after checking with local environmentalist groups, I learned that the city's water and air were heavily polluted and not likely to be cleaned up for a decade.

Recently I went through the process of looking for a new car. After visits to nine different dealerships, multiple test drives, and review of consumer reports' analyses and National Highway Transportation Safety Administration tests, I was finally able to make an informed decision.

Finding the right nursing home is certainly as equally complex as the aforementioned examples, yet it is often given short shrift by abdicating the decision to a third party such as a social worker or discharge planner. In my judgment this is not a good idea because you and your loved one must live with the consequences of the decision, not the third party.

For most people, the process of finding a nursing home for long-term care should be akin to moving into a new home in a new community, that is, two major steps that no one would undertake in a cavalier manner. Indeed, it is important to reemphasize here that going into a nursing home is not like going into a hospital, where patients are whirled through a revolving door before anyone knows his or her name. A new nursing-home resident is the new kid on the block in a small, tightly knit community of several hundred people, most of whom reside in the community twenty-four hours a day, and others of whom work in the community eight hours a day. The search for the right nursing home is hard work. It requires learning about those who reside in the nursing home; about those who attend to the needs of the residents; and about those who manage, control, and implement the policies and procedures of the home.

## Selecting a Location

When I was living in Massachusetts, a friend who lived in my community asked for my advice about a nursing home for his mother, who still lived in his hometown of Philadelphia. I responded, assuming he was asking about homes in our part of New England, but I was wrong. He wanted to know about options in Philadelphia, because, as he explained, his mother's connections were there and his brother still lived in a neighboring community. I provided several names in the Philadelphia area and also suggested that he and his family consider the Massachusetts options I had first identified. Apparently my counsel had an impact, because several days later, he approached me for more information about the Massachusetts homes.

This vignette illustrates two of the most common reasons people appear to select a particular location: current residence and proximity to family. Current residence is a powerful force because it seems to minimize the separation from a familiar environment. Those who move into a local nursing home are likely to find themselves among former acquaintances or perhaps classmates. Because they are locals, they can easily continue some of their community activities and interests, which would be disrupted with a move to a more distant location. George T., a man who was widowed for many years before dying at the age of ninety-one, illustrates my point. Until his last days, despite being confined to a wheelchair, he remained active in his Masonic lodge, going to weekly meetings and other outings via transportation provided by the nursing home and the Masons.

Also, it should be reiterated that a significant percentage of nursing-home residents wind up in a long-term-care facility after a hospitalization (with that hospitalization most often occurring in the local community). The job of the discharge planner is to place the hospital patient in an acceptable nursing home as quickly as possible, while in general, discharge planners working with a number of local nursing homes for a short-term placement are not necessarily focusing on the next step, that is, a long-term stay. Additionally, because of changes in the health system generated by what is known as Obamacare and after 2016 the uncertainty raised by President Trump, the health system is in flux over "accountable care organizations (ACOs)." These ACOs essentially mean that in some instances hospitals will be financially responsible for episodes of care whether that care is provided in a hospital, nursing home, or through home-care services. Along with this responsibility of the hospital comes the power of the hospital to direct the consumer into a nursing home with which they have a contract. In the best of worlds, the consumer will know beforehand that the course of his or her hospitalization may also involve a stay at a particular nursing home—not necessarily the one he or she would normally choose.

This ACO issue is still evolving; I anticipate that they are slowly dying, but it is something for consumers to keep in mind because once a person is in a particular nursing home, a transfer to a second home is difficult and highly unlikely. Additionally, it may be ill advised. The term that social workers and researchers use for this transfer situation is "transfer trauma"—that is, the trauma of transferring is so great that elderly people, once they have adjusted to a facility, simply do not wish to move even if the next home would be significantly better.

This point was emphasized for me in Cleveland where I visited a nursing home that was superb in every respect except that it had a long waiting list. In a neighboring city, I visited one of the most crowded, shabby, and poorly staffed homes that I have ever seen. Here I learned that many of the residents in this third-rate home had been on the waiting list for the first home but had chosen not to go there when space became available for them. It appeared that the residents and their families had made their adjustment to this unsatisfactory place and did not want to go through the difficulties of a second move.

The other major reason for selecting a particular location is the proximity of close relatives, usually children. Moving close to children may come with the cost of severing long-term neighborly relationships, but it does have the benefit of ensuring family contact. The M. family, for example, decided to move both the mother and the father, who lived in suburban Chicago, into a nursing home several hundred miles from the Windy City but within a two-hour drive of three of the four children and a twenty-five-minute drive of one child. The parents, who had been active church members, found a hospitable environment in their new home, which was operated by their same denomination. In commenting on this new arrangement, one of the M. children noted that, after years of confusion and racing back home every time one of the parents became ill, there was a new orderliness and harmony in their relationship. Also, after years of worrying about phone calls in the night, they could finally sleep, knowing their parents were being cared for properly in an excellent institution.

Each family needs to work out its own solution, clarifying which location would be in the best interests of all parties. However, it is important to recognize that there are options in terms of locations, and while some homes are geographically restrictive in terms of the catchment area they will serve, many are willing to consider applicants from anywhere in the country, particularly if that applicant has a local connection.

## Using the Internet to Search and Research Nursing Homes

Thanks to the US government's Centers for Medicare & Medicaid Services (CMS), consumers have a powerful range of tools available for both finding nursing-home options as well as investigating the available choices. The central tool for this analysis is found on the following website: https://www.medicare.gov/nursinghomecompare/search.html?. This website presents a comprehensive set of core statistics about virtually every nursing home in the United States. However, it should be clear that the data the consumer has available from this site is a starting point for choosing a nursing home simply because the data is always slightly out of date. What one views on the Internet should be a source of consumer education as well as a starting point for making a decision.

## What You Can Learn from www.medicare.gov

Basically the government's website will assist the consumer to find a nursing home in a community or other larger geographic area. A quite valuable aspect of the site is that it allows the consumer to compare a variety of nursing homes on the basis of health-inspection results, nursing-home staffing data, quality measures, and fire-safety reports. All this is summarized by the government using a five-star system—much like a hotel or restaurant guide. Once again, a caution, that is, what is being viewed is a snapshot in time and that time has occurred months or perhaps even more than a year earlier.

## The US Government's Nursing Home Compare Site

The following includes portions of text from the Medicare website's subsection "Nursing Homes Compare." This site provides an enormous amount of information about all Medicare- and Medicaid-certified homes in the United States. Because some of the details are overwhelming such as reading the actual inspection report (which is available), much of the useful consumer information is provided in a shortened form.

Additionally, as an ultimate summary of the text, a five-star system is used to rate the components of the inspection. Somewhat like the system used by many hotel and travel sites, a five-star rating is the best with a one star being the lowest. While these ratings are enormously helpful in making any decision, they do have some limitations that I will discuss at the end of this chapter. The following sections (in italics) are direct excerpts from the www.Medicare.gov website's subsection "Nursing Homes Compare."

***How can Nursing Home Compare help you?***

*Nursing Home Compare allows you to find and compare nursing homes certified by Medicare and Medicaid. This website contains quality of resident care and staffing information for more than 15,000 nursing homes around the country. Nursing homes provide skilled care to people who can't be cared for at home and need 24-hour nursing care. Skilled care includes skilled nursing or rehabilitation services to manage, observe, or assess a resident's care. Examples of skilled care include occupational therapy, wound care, intravenous (IV) therapies, and physical therapy. You can learn more about other types of long-term care facilities here.*

*The information on Nursing Home Compare can help you learn:*

- *How nursing homes have performed on health and fire safety inspections*
- *How the nursing home is staffed with nurses and other healthcare providers*
- *How well nursing homes care for their residents*

*Information on Nursing Home Compare is not an endorsement or advertisement for any nursing home and should be considered carefully. Use the information you find on this website along with other information you gather about nursing homes. Talk to your doctor or other healthcare provider about the information on Nursing Home Compare. If possible, visit the nursing homes you are considering or have someone visit for you. You can also use the Nursing Home Checklist to get important information to help you make decisions about what nursing home best meets you or your family member's needs. Read more about finding a nursing home.*

*Note: Nursing homes are not included on Nursing Home Compare if they are not certified by Medicare or Medicaid. Those nursing homes may be licensed by a state. For information about nursing homes not on Nursing Home Compare, contact your State Survey Agency.*

***What information can you get about nursing homes?***

*Nursing Home Compare provides details on nursing homes across the country. This includes nursing home inspection results, staffing levels, enforcement actions that the federal government have taken against the nursing homes and how well nursing home residents were treated in specific areas of care.*

***General information about nursing homes***

*When you search for nursing homes using Nursing Home Compare, you can find general information on more than 15,000 Medicare- and Medicaid-participating nursing homes, including:*

- ***Nursing home name & address****, including street, city, state, and ZIP code, as well as the distance from the ZIP code where you based your search.*
- ***Whether the nursing home participates in Medicare, Medicaid or both.*** *The nursing homes included on Nursing Home Compare are certified by Medicare or Medicaid. Those that aren't certified nursing homes aren't included on Nursing Home Compare. For information about nursing homes not on Nursing Home Compare, contact your State Survey Agency.*
- ***Whether the nursing home is within a Continuing Care Retirement Community (CCRC).*** *Continuing Care Retirement Communities (CCRC) offer multiple housing options and levels of care. A nursing home is typically the most service-intensive housing option. Residents may move from one level to another based on their particular needs, while typically still remaining in the CCRC.*
- ***If the nursing home is located within a hospital.*** *Some individuals need a more intensive level of care that can only be provided in a hospital setting. Some Skilled Nursing Facilities (SNF) are located within a hospital, allowing residents to be transferred to an acute care setting more easily if necessary.*
- ***If the nursing home has a resident and family council.*** *Resident and family councils can help communications with staff. Federal law requires nursing homes to allow councils to be set up by residents and families. If a nursing home doesn't have a resident and family council, ask the administrator why. Ask to talk with a council president to get a sense of how the nursing home has acted on their concerns.*
- ***Type of ownership.*** *Nursing homes can be owned by for-profit or non-profit entities. The entities themselves can range from sole proprietorships to complex multi-facility corporations. Many nursing homes are owned or managed by religious organizations or government agencies.*
- ***Whether the nursing home has submitted staffing data through the Payroll-Based Journal (PBJ) reporting program.*** *The program*

*aims to improve the accuracy of publically reported staffing information for nursing homes.*

***Star ratings***

*Nursing Home Compare features a star rating system that gives each facility a rating between 1 and 5 stars. The nursing home star ratings come from:*

- *Health inspections*
- *Staffing*
- *Quality of resident care measures*

*The Centers for Medicare & Medicaid Services (CMS) calculates a star rating for each of these 3 sources, along with an overall rating.*

***Why is this information important?***

*Nursing homes vary in the quality of care and services they provide to their residents. Health inspection results, staffing data, and quality of resident care information are 3 important ways to measure the quality of a nursing homes. This information, combined in the star rating, gives you a "snapshot" of the quality of each nursing home.*

***Using the star rating with other information***

*The star rating system can give you important information and help you compare nursing homes by topics you consider most important, but isn't a substitute for visiting the nursing home.*

***Health & fire safety inspections***

*Nursing Home Compare collects information on health and fire safety inspections.*

***Health inspections***

*Certified nursing homes must meet over 180 standards set by the federal government to protect residents. Examples of these standards include:*

- *Hiring enough quality staff to provide adequate care*
- *Managing medications properly*
- *Protecting residents from physical and mental abuse*
- *Storing and preparing food properly*

*State survey agencies conduct health inspections about once a year on behalf of the federal government, and may inspect nursing homes more often if the nursing home is performing poorly if there are complaints or facility reported incidents. The health inspection team consists of trained inspectors, including at least one registered nurse.*

*Using the federal government's standards, the inspection team looks at many aspects of life in the nursing home including, but not limited to:*

- *The care of residents and the processes used to give that care*
- *How the staff and residents interact*
- *The nursing home environment*

*Inspectors also review the residents' clinical records, interview residents and family members, as well as caregivers and administrative staff. The health inspection measures listed on the website show the results from the last 3 yearly inspections and the last 3 years of inspections from complaints.*

***Fire safety inspections***

*Fire safety specialists inspect nursing homes to measure if a nursing home meets Life Safety Code (LSC) standards set by CMS, based on codes established by the National Fire Protection Association (NFPA). The fire safety inspection covers building design and construction and operational features designed to provide safety from fire, smoke, electrical failures, and gas leaks.*

***Why is health & fire safety inspection information important?***

*To be part of the Medicare and Medicaid programs, nursing homes must meet certain requirements set by the federal government to protect residents, including those about fire safety. If a nursing home has no citations, it means that it met federal standards at time of its inspections.*

*While reading these reports, keep in mind that the quality of a nursing home may get much better or much worse in a short period of time. These changes can occur when a nursing home's administrator or ownership changes, or when a nursing home's finances suddenly change.*

*Each nursing home that provides services to people with Medicare or Medicaid must make the results of its last full inspection available at the nursing home for anyone to review. Nursing Home Compare shows all reports from the last 3 years.*

***What are citations?***

*If an inspection team finds that a nursing home doesn't meet a specific federal standard, it issues a* ***citation.*** *The federal government may impose penalties on nursing homes for serious citations or for citations that the nursing home doesn't correct for a long time.*

***What are complaints?***

*Inspectors also may visit a nursing home when a complaint is registered about a nursing home. Nursing Home Compare includes health citations that result from inspections about a complaint.*

***Staffing***

*Each nursing home annually reports its staffing hours to the Centers for Medicare & Medicaid Services (CMS). CMS calculates a ratio of staffing hours per resident day and reports those ratios on Nursing Home Compare.*

*These types of staff are included in the nursing home staffing information that is collected by CMS:*

- *Registered Nurse (RN)*
- *Licensed Practical Nurse (LPN) and Licensed Vocational Nurse (LVN)*
- *Certified Nursing Assistant (CNA)*
- *Physical Therapist (PT)*

*Staffing hours per resident per day is the total number of hours worked by the staff member(s) divided by the total number of residents. It doesn't necessarily show the number of nursing staff present at any given time, or reflect the amount of care given to any one resident.*

***What are the differences between the types of staff?***
***Registered nurses and licensed practical and vocational nurses***
*Registered nurses (RNs) are responsible for the overall delivery of care to the residents. Licensed practical and vocational nurses (LPNs/LVNs) provide care under the direction of an RN. Together, RNs and LPNs/LVNs make sure each resident's plan of care is being followed and their needs are being met. Nursing homes must have at least one RN for at least 8 straight hours a day, 7 days a week, and either an RN or LPN/LVN on duty 24 hours per day. Certain states may have additional staffing requirements. Nurses must be licensed in the state where they practice.*

***Certified nursing assistants***
*Certified nursing assistants (CNAs) work under the direction of a licensed nurse to assist residents with activities of daily living like eating, bathing, grooming, dressing, transferring, and toileting. All full time CNAs must have completed a competency evaluation program or nurse assistant training within 4 months of their permanent employment. They must also pursue continuing education each year. CNAs provide care to nursing home residents 24 hours per day, 7 days a week.*

***Physical therapists***
*Physical therapists (PTs) help residents improve their movement and manage their pain. PTs test muscle strength, the amount of flexibility in joints, and the resident's ability to walk or move. PTs often work with other providers, like doctors, nurses, and occupational therapists to create individualized therapy plans to address and restore the resident's physical function and well-being. All states license PTs. The amount of physical therapy service hours depends on the needs of the resident.*

***Note**: Each state may have its own specific education and training requirements for nursing home staff.*

***Why is staffing information important?***

*Federal law requires all nursing homes to provide enough staff to safely care for residents. However, there is no current federal standard for the best nursing home staffing levels. The staffing rating takes into account differences in the levels of residents' care needs in each nursing home. For example, a nursing home with residents that have more health problems would be expected to have more nursing staff than a nursing home where the residents need less health care.*

***Quality of resident care***

*The nursing homes that the Centers for Medicare & Medicaid Services (CMS) certifies regularly report clinical information about each of their residents. CMS uses this information to measure parts of nursing home care quality, like if residents have gotten their flu shots, are in pain, or are losing weight. These measures are often called the "quality of resident care", and Medicare posts each nursing home's scores for these measures on Nursing Home Compare. By comparing scores, you can see how nursing homes may be different from each other.*

*Nursing Home Compare has two different types of quality of resident care measures: short- and long-stay resident quality measures.*

***Short-stay quality of resident care measures***

*Short-stay resident quality measures show the average quality of resident care in a nursing home for those who stayed in a nursing home for less than 101 days. Short-stay residents often are those recovering from surgery or being discharged from a hospital stay. Many short-stay residents get care in a nursing home until they're able to go back home or to the community.*

The first quality measure considered is related to mobility: "The percentage of short-stay nursing home residents of all ages who got better at moving around during their stay." The goal is improvement in this area, so the homes that show a higher percentage of patient improvement are more highly rated.

A second and critically important measure is percentage of short-stay residents who are re-hospitalized for an unplanned admission after a nursing-home stay of thirty days or less. The theory here is that when a readmission occurs, the nursing home has failed to properly do its job of rehabilitation. Generally neither the nursing home nor the hospital wants to see these readmissions. If a nursing home has a higher-than-average percentage of these readmissions, it means that either they are not doing a good job or alternatively they are handling the toughest cases that perhaps should not have been initially accepted by the home. A similar measure relates to nursing-home transfers to emergency rooms. Here too a percentage that is higher than the average should set up warning flags for prospective clients.

Other quality measures that Medicare identifies as important are the percentage of residents who need and receive flu immunizations, percentage of patients in severe pain, and percentage of patients with new pressure ulcers or pressure ulcers that have gotten worse or those with urinary-tract infections. While they are not identified by the government, another concern should be falls.

In my judgment the pressure ulcers, urinary-tract infections, psychotic drug overutilization, and falls are at the top of the list of problems in many nursing homes. The extent to which a home has protocols to deal with these issues is often the extent to which these problems are mitigated.

Finally, a word about patient abuse. The elderly and infirmed are prime targets for abuse by staff, volunteers, visitors, and other residents and patients. Estimates of abuse range from one in six to one in ten residents who may be abused or neglected. While every state has antiabuse legislation, it is up to those selecting a facility to be alert to any signs that the residents are being victimized. In chapter 11 I write about interviewing residents in the nursing homes under consideration and the need to use all your senses to discern whether the residents are being treated in a manner that you wish your loved one to be treated.

***Long-stay quality of resident care measures***

*Long-stay resident quality measures show the average quality of care for certain care areas in a nursing home for those who stayed in a nursing home for*

*101 days or more. Residents in a nursing home for a long-stay are usually not healthy enough to leave a nursing home and can't live at home or in a community setting. These residents may be older and have more serious health issues.*

The Medicare data analyze numerous measures of quality all presented as percentages. The first measure is that of long-stay residents experiencing one or more falls with major injuries such as bone fractures, joint dislocations, or head injuries. Medicare then indicates that lower percentages are better, but it offers no baseline data goal. In an illustration that I present later in this chapter, I show a comparison between three institutions on quality measures.

Other data presented by the Medicare quality survey include health issues where lower percentages among long-stay residents are considered better because they indicate a more active and aggressive staff working to prevent or solve problems common to people who are elderly and institutionalized. These health issues are urinary-tract infections, reported moderate to severe pain, pressure ulcers, significant bowel and bladder-control problems, catheters being used and left in the bladder, use of physical restraints, worsening independence of resident, increased number of residents who have need for assistance in activities of daily living, residents who lose too much weight, residents who have symptoms of depression, and residents receiving antianxiety, hypnotic, or antipsychotic drugs. There are also two categories where "higher" is better than "lower." These are the percentage of residents who have received flu shots and those who have received the pneumonia vaccine.

A visit to the Medicare.gov website provides additional information of each of these measures. For the consumer, though the key is still identifying homes in your community, comparing them with basic information, and then doing site visits.

## Using the Medicare Nursing-Home-Compare Website: An Illustration

To begin the process of investigating a nursing home, all that is necessary is for the consumer to go to Medicare.gov and scroll down to the "Find nursing homes" on the left sidebar and click on it. On the next screen, enter a zip code or location, and click on "Search." This brings up a screen that provides a summary of information on all the nursing homes in the area of the zip code, including address and distance from the entered zip code.

For example, when I use my home zip code, I am provided with a total of seventy-seven homes within twenty-five miles from the center of my neighborhood. In fact, there are only two homes within my zip code, with the remainder ranging from three miles away to more than twenty-four miles. While some of these distant homes are quite good, they are also, depending on traffic, between forty-five minutes and an hour away by car (and dramatically longer with public transportation). The Medicare.gov website allows users to compare information about three homes at a time. To do this, click the "Add to compare" at the bottom of the summary of each home. After the three homes are selected, scroll to the bottom of the entire document, and click on "compare." This then generates twelve pages of material for review. This initial page provides summary information, including the name and address of the home, distance from the reference zip code, and the overall star rating along with a statement whether that rating is much below average, below average, average, above average, or much above average. There are then columns for the health-inspection rating, staffing rating, and quality-measure rating. The data are all presented in table format so that one can easily compare any three homes and also compare the homes with state and national data.

The first tab provides information on health inspections of the facility. It also reviews the last full inspection report that typically has occurred within the previous twelve months. It provides information on deficiencies at the home and also provides comparisons with state and national averages.

Unfortunately not available is detailed information on environmental deficiencies and whether the deficiencies have been corrected and whether these deficiencies resulted in minimal harm or potential for actual harm and how many residents were affected. There is also a section on building service equipment deficiencies, electrical deficiencies, and, most important, complaints and incidents. When there are even a handful of complaints and incidences that affect any residents, and result in potential or actual harm, a consumer should be alert to other potential issues.

The next tab is titled "Fire Safety Inspections." In examining a number of homes under this tab, I found no useful information.

The following tab "Staffing" is invaluable. Under this tab are the following subcategories: total number of licensed nurse staff hours per day, which is further segmented by RN hours per resident per day and LPN/LVN per resident per day; CNA hours per resident per day; and physical therapy staff hours per resident per day. This section also provides state averages and national averages in each of these staffing categories. The best nursing homes operate staffing levels in all categories that exceed state and national averages.

The next tab presents the details of quality measures. These data can be viewed in the form of tables or graphs. Additionally, the data are divided by short-stay residents or long-stay residents. As noted earlier in this chapter, different components of quality are examined including the following: the percent of long-stay residents experiencing one or more falls with major injury, the percent of long-stay residents with a urinary-tract infection, the percent of long-stay residents who self-report moderate to severe pain, the percent of long stay high-risk residents with pressure ulcers, the percent of long-stay low-risk patients who lose control of their bowels or bladder, the percent of long-stay residents who have or had a catheter inserted and left in their bladder, the percent of long-stay residents who are physically restrained, the percent of long-stay residents whose need for help with daily activities has increased, the percent of long-stay residents who lose too much weight, the percent of long-stay residents who have depressive symptoms, the percent of long-stay residents assessed and given appropriately the seasonal influenza vaccine, the percent of long-stay residents assessed and given appropriately the pneumococcal vaccine, and the percent of long-stay residents who received an antipsychotic medication.

All these quality measures are presented for each specific nursing home and then compared with state and national averages. These averages give a sense of whether the nursing homes of interest are in or out of the ballpark. For example, two of the most important quality measures (in my opinion) are pressure ulcers and falls.

By way of illustration, I compared three nursing homes (A, B, and C) on two of the many quality issues, that is, pressure ulcers and urinary-tract infections. On a comparative basis, nursing home A had 0.0 residents with pressure ulcer issues, home B had 11.8 percent of their residents with pressure ulcer issues, and home C had 8.0 percent of their residents with problems. The statewide average was 5.9 percent and nationwide the number was 5.6 percent. To me these data suggest a serious problem with the nursing care and nursing protocols at homes B and C. Looking at the urinary-tract infection issue, I found that A had a rate of 3.1 percent, B had a rate of 7.1 percent, and C was at 3.8 percent. Statewide the rate was 3.6 percent and nationwide 3.4 percent. In my judgment nursing home B should be eliminated from consideration, great care should be exercised if C is of interest, and nursing home A looks like the best option. However, even with A I would ask questions about their protocols for preventing urinary-tract infections.

The last tab has to do with penalties. When a nursing home is found to have deficiencies found by surveyors that place residents in immediate jeopardy, or residents have actually be harmed, the government can and often does impose monetary penalties on the nursing home that can include fines and suspension of admissions.

However, this system of penalties is in flux. For example, on November 24, 2017, the Centers for Medicare & Medicaid Services issued a memorandum to State Survey Agency Directors that ordered a temporary eighteen-month delay on the use of remedies such as civil money penalties and denials of payments for new admissions for certain deficiencies that previously might have resulted in fines or denial of admissions. Other changes outlined in the November memo included freezing star ratings between November 28, 2017, and November 27, 2018.

Additionally, earlier in the year, CMS basically limited the amount that can be levied in fines and set up an internal systems of oversight for these fines.

For consumers when penalties (fines) represent a significant amount of money such as more than $10,000.00, it usually means that there are or were serious problems that weren't resolved within the time allotted for their rectification. Other penalties such as suspension of payments or not allowing new admissions send up warning signals to knowledgeable consumers.

***What to keep in mind when using quality of resident care measures***

*The quality of resident care measures on Nursing Home Compare aren't benchmarks, thresholds, guidelines, or standards of care, and aren't appropriate for use in a lawsuit. They are based on the average quality of care given to all the residents in a nursing home and don't detail a single resident's experience.*

*Most of these quality measures show residents' health in the 7 days before the assessment was done. This means that the quality measures may not show the residents' health during the entire time between assessments.*

***Penalties***

*Centers for Medicare & Medicaid Services (CMS) may impose penalties on a nursing home when there's a serious health or fire safety citation or if the nursing home fails to correct a citation for a long period of time. For example, Medicare may issue a fine, deny payment to the nursing home, assign a temporary manager, or install a state monitor. Nursing Home Compare only lists penalties that have been imposed in the last 3 years.*

***What are the types of penalties on Nursing Home Compare?***

*There are 2 types of penalties reported on Nursing Home Compare:*

- ***Fines**: Fines may be imposed once per citation or each day until the nursing home corrects the citation.*
- ***Payment denials**: During a payment denial, the government stops Medicare or Medicaid payments to the nursing home for new residents until the nursing home corrects the citation.*

***Why is this information important?***

*If the nursing home doesn't correct these problems, Medicare will end its agreement with the nursing home. This means the nursing home is no longer certified to provide and be paid for care to people with Medicare or Medicaid. Residents with Medicare or Medicaid who are living in the home at the time of the termination will be moved to a different nursing home that is still certified by CMS.*

On an earlier version of the nursing home compare website, the Centers for Medicare and & Medicaid Services (CMS) offered the following cautionary words that in my opinion are enormously important:

*Caution:* *No rating system can address all the important considerations that go into a decision about which nursing home may be best for a particular person. Examples include the extent to which specialty care is provided (such as specialized rehabilitation of dementia care) or how easy it will be for family members to visit a nursing home resident. As such visits can improve both the residents quality of life and quality of care, it may often be better to select a nursing home that is very close, compared to a higher rated nursing home that would be far away. Consumers should therefore use the website only together with other sources of information for nursing homes (including a visit to the nursing home) and state or local organizations (such as local advocacy groups and the State Ombudsman program).*

Finally it is imperative that the consumer dig deeply to learn about any given home because the available CMS information is being severely curtailed as a result of new rules and policies being promulgated by the Trump administration.

## Four Caveats about the Medicare.gov Data

### Still Photos and Old Data

All data posted on the Internet are old data. Sometimes it is a year or more old, sometimes a few weeks. Many things may have occurred since the previous survey including a total change of staff including organizational leadership such as the administrator or director of nursing. Think of the data you get on the Internet as the first step in your analysis.

## Significant Issues with the Five-Star System

In March 2012 the US General Accounting Office issued a report to Congress about the five-star system. This report reached the following conclusion:

*In an attempt to make information on nursing home quality easier for consumers to understand and use, and to help improve provider quality, CMS developed and implemented the Five-Star System in 8 months using information that was readily available. This was a significant step toward increasing the transparency of information important to consumers, but for CMS to sustain the Five-Star System over time, the agency will need to continue making a concerted effort. CMS has made some efforts to update the Five-Star System as it reviews the system's underlying components to identify potential ways to improve the system over time. However, there can be significant challenges to ensuring that the Five-Star System remains useful and valid over time, especially when the components of that system continue to evolve. While CMS has identified efforts it intends to make to improve the Five-Star System, the agency has not strategically planned how to carry out these efforts, such as outlining the milestones and timelines that will help ensure that progress is being made. In addition, CMS has not clearly identified how each of its planned efforts will help achieve the goals of the Five-Star System. As a result, CMS may not know how it will prioritize and best leverage its available resources to implement these efforts and achieve the goals of the Five-Star System. Additionally, during this period of fiscal constraint, these strategic planning practices can help CMS to better anticipate and make resource allocation decisions that minimize the effect of funding constraints on accomplishing the goals of the Five-Star System.*

Additionally, as noted earlier, the star system has effectively been put on hold through November 2018, and beyond that date its future is uncertain.

## The Best Survey Is Your Own Multiple Field Trips—*Trips, Not Trip!*

Nothing is a substitute for actually visiting the nursing home, touring, speaking with staff and residents, and observing. In another chapter I will provide a detailed approach about doing these surveys for yourself. *Unfortunately one visit will not do the trick.* It is absolutely imperative that a smart consumer spends at least as much time searching for a nursing home as he or she would while buying a car, piece of jewelry, or shirt!

## Location-Location-Location

As I discussed earlier, one of the most important factors in insuring a successful nursing-home experience for a loved one is family and friends visiting with great frequency. These visits are important for the psychological well-being of the resident, that is, they know they haven't be abandoned. Additionally these visits are essential for keeping the staff on their toes vis-à-vis a loved one. The frequent visitors, particularly if they are family members, will notice issues that may need to be dealt with and will often give voice to problems that the resident is reluctant to bring up.

Because of the overarching importance of frequent visitors, it is important to find a home that is accessible for visitors—oftentimes one that can be reached with public transportation.

Finally, while I am reluctant to even suggest that a resident be placed in anything but the best available home, sometimes best may also mean a place where the resident is not isolated from family and friends.

Recently I had lunch with the single, retired man whose mother had been admitted to an excellent nursing home in the Bronx, New York, several years earlier. When I asked this gentleman where he lived, he told me that he had lived most of his life in Brooklyn, but after his mother went into the nursing home, he moved to a condo in the Bronx that was about three miles away from her nursing home. He did this because he simply wanted to visit his mom frequently. He then went on to tell me that in his time visiting he had gotten to know the nursing and other staff and he wasn't afraid to speak up when something was not going properly with his mother. He said that in observing the other residents and seeing how his mother was treated, he was absolutely certain that his regular presence and essential oversight of his mother's care were crucial to the quality of care that she was receiving. I absolutely agree, and that is why I emphasize the importance of location!

# CHAPTER 11

## The Preliminary Nursing-Home Visit

Having selected several possible nursing homes, the next step is to visit these homes because there is simply no substitute for a personal inspection of the homes. This chapter deals with a number of crucial questions, including why a preliminary visit is necessary, who should go, how to arrange for the visit, what to expect from the nursing home, whom to interview, what questions to ask, what to look for, and how to evaluate your findings.

### Purposes of the Preliminary Visit

Just as a young physician cannot learn to be a surgeon simply by reading textbooks, it is impossible to learn about specific nursing homes without investing the time to visit them. The central purpose of this preliminary visit is to give a potential resident and his or her family a chance to decide whether a particular home is worth a second and more thorough look, but the visit also can serve a number of other objectives. Perhaps the most important objective is to clarify whether a nursing home is really the most reasonable alternative for a loved one. By seeing several nursing homes and carefully observing the facilities, staff, residents, and programs, and getting a sense of the rhythm of the day, everyone will be in a better position to understand the consequences of a move into a nursing home.

The preliminary visit is also an opportunity for clarifying such issues as the cost of the nursing-home care, the availability of private rooms or rooms for married couples, and the types of specialized programs set up for residents with dementia or Alzheimer's disease. The visit also provides an opportunity for developing skills in interviewing staff and residents and observing life in a nursing home. Finally, during the visit, you can obtain helpful material such as residents' handbooks, contracts, and annual reports if you did not receive them in advance.

## The Preliminary-Visit Team

It is best if more than one person makes the preliminary visits, and perhaps as many as three or four people *inspect*. If possible, this group should include the prospective resident as well as some close friends or relatives. Frequently, the prospective resident is not available or is not well enough to make the trip, in which case a family may have to accept the responsibility for a visit.

There are two major reasons to send a team rather than one person: (1) with the team approach, no individual needs to take the entire responsibility for the decision or has to be the focus for negative feelings generated about a nursing-home placement and (2) two heads are better than one. There is much to see on a visit, and two or more people are likely to observe more and have useful and complementary insights. The value of the team approach will become clear once the group has reconvened after the visit to share impressions of the home.

## Arranging the Visit

Although Medicare/Medicaid inspectors make unannounced visits and the nursing home is obligated by law to respond to their demands, it is wise to make an appointment for a preliminary visit. Advance scheduling allows the home to arrange for the various interviews (suggested in the next section) and also to give the staff a chance to plan your visit when it is most convenient for them. The value of this is that you are an expected guest, and if the home is properly responsive, you will not be rushed through the visit. While some might argue that advance notice provides the nursing home with a chance to put its best foot forward so you may not get an accurate picture of it, I do not put much weight on this position. Most nursing homes are busy places, and they simply do not have the time or resources to spiff up the premises for just one set of interviewers.

In planning for this preliminary visit, you should be prepared to answer several questions from the home about the prospective resident and perhaps about finances. Additionally, ask the home to make arrangements for your group to tour the facility, talk with some residents, and meet with the key members of the staff who will be responsible for delivering care to the future resident. The accompanying Preliminary-Visit Arrangement Checklist will help organize these aspects of a visit.

## PRELIMINARY VISIT—ARRANGEMENT CHECKLIST

Nursing Home Name
Phone Number
Directions to Facility
Date of Visit

Part I: [Have this information about the prospective resident ready before calling the home]

1. Name of prospective resident
2. Date of birth
3. General health status

Any specific medical problems? Any mental health problems?

4. What type of help, if any, is needed for any of the following activities:

Bathing/Dressing/Toileting/Transferring (moving from bed to chair, tub, or toilet)/Continence (bowel and bladder control)/Eating

5. How will the cost of nursing-home care be financed—private pay, insurance, Medicare, Medicaid?

Part II: [Visit plans]

1. Be prepared to tell the home who will be coming on the visit and their relationships to the prospective resident.
2. Be prepared with several alternative dates.
3. Tell the person arranging the visit that you would like to meet with the following people:
    a. The administrator
    b. The director of nursing
    c. The director of social services
    d. The activities director
4. Tell the home you also wish to meet with several residents preferably ones who are about the same age and sex as your prospective resident.
5. Tell the home you wish to tour the facility and see a resident's room, the dining areas, the activities and therapy areas, and other commons areas.
6. Ask the home if it is possible for you to eat a meal there at your own expense.
7. Ask the home for a residents' handbook, contracts, annual report, or other public-relations documents prior to your visit.

## The Interviewees and Areas of Inquiry

The visit to the nursing home is primarily a series of interviews and observations. This section identifies those who should be interviewed, what questions should be asked of them, and why. The next section provides some suggestions concerning observations.

## Interviewing the Administrator

The administrator is responsible for the day-to-day management of the nursing home and has a great deal of influence over the entire atmosphere of the institution. Some administrators keep themselves ensconced in their offices and learn about the home through written or oral reports delivered by subordinates. Others have adopted the "MBWA" approach—Management by Walking Around. This second type of administrator tends to know every nook and cranny of the home and seems genuinely interested in the welfare of the residents. Indeed, touring a facility with such administrators is exhausting merely because they stop to greet each resident and their families. However, the exhaustion is well worth it when one recognizes that the caring atmosphere created by this kind of manager goes a long way toward creating a non-institutional feel in a nursing home.

The agenda for the meeting with the administrator has several elements. First, it is important to obtain background information on the administrator and, by extension, a sense of the commitment of the institution to top-notch administration. An institution committed to first-class management is likely to have an administrator who has a master's degree in some area of health administration, gerontology, human-services administration, business administration, or social work. An alternative might be someone with a background in a technical and clinical specialty, such as nursing, physical therapy, or occupational therapy, plus training for nursing-home licensure. Finally, as in other fields, it is important not to be influenced solely by the presence or absence of a person's academic achievements—there are plenty of excellent nursing-home administrators who, through years of experience, have grown into the job and become models of excellence.

On the other hand, a warning flag should go up when an administrator's background and training seem inappropriate to the job. While the individual may indeed be quite competent, one must question the commitment of the owner or board that hires such a person. For example, I visited one home where the administrator had been a used-car salesperson for ten years before becoming an activities assistant and then activities director at a small nursing home. Armed with his four years of experience in activities and a new nursing-home license, he was able to obtain the job of administrator in another small nursing home. While it was clear that he was quite a nice person, and no doubt an excellent salesman for the nursing home, it was equally clear that he was merely a front man for the absentee-owner, who ran the home from the other end of a phone line. In my opinion, such people are hired by owners who need to meet the letter of the law—that is, a state requirement for an on-premises licensed administrator—but not the spirit of the law, which calls for a professionally trained independent administrator.

The administrator can be a source of considerable information about the facility, and the Administrator Questionnaire Preliminary Visit (AQPV) should be used as the principal tool for gathering the necessary information about both the administrator and the institution.

The first group of questions focuses on the home's ownership and governance—who is truly in charge. As already noted, it is my judgment that to a major extent, organizational anatomy is destiny. In practice, this means that one can tell a great deal about the functioning of a home by learning about its ownership and how that ownership chooses to govern the home.

The second set of questions speaks to the background and qualifications of the administrator in order to plumb the commitment of the home to management excellence.

The third set of questions deals with several specific and critical issues. First, it is important for a prospective resident to be aware of the medical supervision of the facility. Most nursing homes contract with someone who has the title of medical director and spends very little time in the home, perhaps two to four hours a week. If the home is a skilled-nursing facility with a significant number of very elderly and sick people, several hours of medical supervision may be too meager. If the new nursing-home resident is likely to need more intense medical supervision, it is important to find a facility with a more extensive medical program.

In response to the question about medical supervision, you are most likely to learn that there is a part-time medical director but that each resident has his or her private physician. This may sound good on paper, but the reality is that most nursing-home residents do not receive much attention from local practitioners, although obviously there are exceptions. The typical story is that the local doctor merely breezes through the home, making perfunctory visits. A related question is whether or not the home employs a geriatric nurse practitioner. Such specially trained nurses, functioning under a physician's supervision, can in many instances provide the necessary on-site medical care required in a nursing home.

The next issue relates to transfers. In the best of situations, a resident would not be moved to another nursing home except for specific clinical reasons or at the request of the resident for social reasons, such as being geographically closer to relatives. The major concern about transfers is economic—that is, does the home transfer people when they run out of private-pay funds? This problem is more likely to occur primarily in the strictly private-pay home that is not Medicare or Medicaid certified. However, some of these homes have policies that provide for "scholarships" to individuals who have been residents and have run out of funds.

The issue that should be explored next is that of any recent deficiencies on the regular Medicare/Medicaid survey. It will be useful to hear the administrator's explanation of why the deficiencies occurred and how the home acted to remedy them.

The last three questions ask the administrator to identify the strengths and weaknesses of the nursing home, to explain the home's philosophy, and to provide an example of how that philosophy is put into practice. While these questions tend to be open-ended, the answers may be very revealing in two ways: (1) they may provide you with an indication of the willingness of the administrator to be candid with you and (2) they may reveal some possible areas for further investigation.

## ADMINISTRATOR QUESTIONNAIRE—PRELIMINARY VISIT

I. Ownership and Governance

A. Is this a for-profit, not-for-profit, or government-owned nursing home?

1. IF FOR-PROFIT:
   a. Who owns this facility? Where are they located?
   b. Is the home part of a chain? If yes, how large a chain?
   c. Are you [the administrator] one of the owners?
   d. Is there a complex ownership structure where the owners cannot even be identified?

2. IF NOT-FOR-PROFIT:
   a. Who is on the governing board of the nursing home?
   b. How do people get on the home's governing board?
   c. Does the home have a particular religious, fraternal, or other special orientation?
   d. How often does the board meet? How often does the board's executive committee meet?

3. IF GOVERNMENT-OWNED:
   a. What agency of government is responsible for the home?
   b. Does the home have a supervisory or governing board?
   c. Who serves on the board? How often does it meet?

II. Administrator's Education and Experience

a. How long have you been a licensed nursing-home administrator?
b. What is your educational background?
c. How long have you been at this nursing home? In what capacity?
d. What other experience have you had in nursing homes?

III. Administrative Issues

a. Who is the nursing home's medical director? How much time per week does he or she spend at the home? Does the home employ a geriatric nurse practitioner?

b. What is the home's policy on transfers? How many people have been transferred to another home in the last year? What were the reasons for the transfers?
c. On the 20___ Medicaid/Medicare certification survey, the following deficiencies were noted. Can you please explain why these deficiencies occurred?
d. What do you see as the strengths and weaknesses of this nursing home?
e. What is the philosophy of the nursing home? Can you provide an example of how that philosophy is put into practice?
f. What nursing-home services are provided by outside vendors? Outside vendors could include management services, clinical services, food services, and housekeeping services (to name a few).

## Interviewing the Nursing Director

The nursing director is a key person in the hierarchy of the nursing home. It is usually the responsibility of the nursing director to recruit and train staff, and the quality of nursing leadership can have an important impact on the quality of care at the home. The interview with the nursing director should result in two types of data for your subsequent analysis: (1) data about the nursing director's personality and style and (2) quantitative data about the nursing organization.

The interview ought to begin with a request for information about the director's experience and education. Although these two items are important, I should note that one of the most sensitive and thoughtful nursing directors I met in my travels was a man who was only two years out of nursing school. Although a neophyte in the world of nursing, he had chosen it as a second career after more than a decade as a successful middle manager in a national corporation. In this individual's case, his skills in management and his commitment to the elderly clearly outweighed his inexperience in nursing.

The next questions are crucial for clarifying the home's nursing picture, specifically vacancies, turnover, wages, and pool (temporary agency) usage.

Vacant positions do not provide nursing care. These proposed questions clarify the stability of the home's staff and the competitiveness of the home in recruiting nurses from a marketplace with a chronic shortage.

The question about pools may be of particular importance. Pool nurses are essentially day workers who fill in when a home has an unanticipated staff shortfall. In the best of situations, pool nurses are rarely used. However, pool nurses are a reality, and the better nursing homes have organized a pool from which to call in nurses who are familiar with the home's routines and can easily jump into the operation. Any home that appears to be excessively dependent on pool nurses should trigger a warning flag.

The last two questions under nursing-department issues focus on nursing-unit assignments and the transfer process. The answers to these questions will indicate the sensitivity of the home to the needs of the residents and give some indicator about the likely future relationship among the home, the resident, and the family. Fundamentally, these questions plumb the issue of whether that relationship is consultative and participatory or autocratic, perhaps dictatorial.

The final set of questions begins with an inquiry into the nature of special-care units at the home and then focuses on nursing deficiencies that may have been reported on the Medicare/Medicaid survey form. By frankly presenting this information, you as an interviewer have an opportunity to clarify any apparent problems with nursing and also to evaluate how the home responds to criticism. The last two questions appear on each of the questionnaires because if several people from the home respond independently to these questions, you as the interviewer eventually will be able to patch together a clear picture of strengths and weaknesses.

## NURSING DIRECTOR QUESTIONNAIRE—PRELIMINARY VISIT

I. Director's Education and Experience
   a. How long have you been director of nursing? What other nursing positions have you held?
   b. What is your educational background?

II. Nursing Department Issues
   a. How many nursing vacancies presently exist?
   b. How much turnover do you experience each year in the nursing department?
   c. Is nursing staff permanently assigned to particular units or do they routinely rotate?
   d. Are pool nurses routinely relied upon? How many pool nurses are typically on each shift?
   e. On the Medicare/Medicaid survey, the following nursing deficiencies were identified. Any comments about those deficiencies?
   f. What is the process for assigning new residents to a particular unit? Once on a particular unit, are residents ever shifted to other units? If yes, what is the transfer process and to what extent is the resident involved in the decision? Is the family involved in the decision?

III. The Home
   a. What do you see as the strengths and weaknesses of this nursing home?
   b. If you could change several important aspects of the nursing home, what would they be?

## Interviewing the Social-Services Director

As with the questionnaire for the nursing director, the first group of questions provides background information concerning the director and data reflecting the home's commitment to the social-service function. The second set of questions elicits what type of support can be expected from the social-work staff for residents and their families.

Of particular importance in this section is the question about anticipated adjustment problems and how the social-services department helps ease this transition. Since the move into a nursing home is traumatic for all parties, it is helpful to have a home that is sensitive to this issue and experienced in dealing with it.

In one particularly touching example, I talked to the son of a resident who told me how a nursing home's social worker had prepared his mother for the arrival of his father, who was being transferred to the home from another facility. The preparations included taking her to the home's beauty shop the day before, helping her into her favorite clothes on the day of his arrival, and arranging for a welcoming committee and party. The son told me this story with tears welling in his eyes. Obviously, he was grateful for the staff who understood the emotional needs of people at such an important time in their lives.

The last set of questions is similar to those addressed to the other interviewees. Specifically, you need to learn why any deficiencies occurred and what was done to remedy them. Finally, there are the questions about strengths and weaknesses.

## SOCIAL-SERVICES DIRECTOR QUESTIONNAIRE—PRELIMINARY VISIT

I. Director's Education and Experience
   a. How long have you been director of social services? What other social-services positions have you held? What is your educational background?

II. Social-Service Department Issues
   a. How many social workers or social-work assistants are employed in the department?
   b. What type of counseling services do you provide to the residents?
   c. What types of services do you provide to the families of residents?
   d. What are the typical problems new residents encounter when they first move into the home, and what type of assistance does the home provide to deal with those problems?

III. The Home in General
   a. On the 20__ Medicare/Medicaid survey report, the following deficiencies were noted in·social services. Could you please explain

what happened to cause these deficiencies and how they were corrected?

b. What do you see as the strengths of the home?
c. What do you see as the weaknesses of the home?

## Interviewing the Activities Director

To a great extent, the quality of life in a nursing home will be affected by the quality of a home's activities department. A trained activities director will probably have well-planned and executed programs. Vibrant, interesting, comprehensive, accessible, and available activity programs will do much to improve life for the residents. However, none of this can take place without staff and frequently also an active volunteer program.

The first two questions are designed to ascertain the commitment of resources that the nursing home is making to an activities program. The next three questions ask for specifics about the programs. Almost every nursing home issues a monthly schedule of activities, obtains the schedule, and studies it. Note how many different kinds of activities are offered at the home. Of these activities, how many are active and how many are passive? How many involve the residents truly interacting with other residents and staff and how many allow the residents simply to be observers? Are there special events that tie together weeks or months? Are there projects such as workshops or theater productions that allow the residents to build self-esteem while enjoying themselves? Finally, does everything end at 2:30 p.m., leaving the residents to fend for themselves in front of a television for the rest of the day?

To a great extent, the activities staff should be part of the total therapeutic team, and question (f) provides an opening to explore how the activities program fits into the rest of the nursing-home environment. Question (g) is similar to one asked in the social-services interview about new residents' adjustment problems. Here again, it would be useful to know what to expect and how insightful and resourceful the staff is at identifying and working out the inevitable adjustment problems.

The last section of this questionnaire includes the standard Medicare/Medicaid deficiency question, along with the strengths-and-weaknesses questions.

**ACTIVITIES DIRECTOR QUESTIONNAIRE—PRELIMINARY VISIT**

I. Activities Department Issues
   a. How many full-time staffers are assigned to the activities department?
   b. How many volunteers work in the activities area?
   c. What is the range of activities programs at the home?
   d. What are the programs during a typical month?
   e. What programs occur on weekends and evenings?
   f. What is the relationship between the activities department and physical therapy, occupational therapy, and social services?
   g. What are the typical problems new residents have in adjusting to the activities programs? What is done in the department to help them deal with these problems?

II. The Home in General
   a. On the 20__ Medicaid/Medicare survey report, the following relevant deficiencies were noted. Could you please explain what happened to cause these deficiencies and how were they corrected?
   b. What do you see as the strengths and weaknesses of the home?

## Meeting with Residents

Nothing will prove to be more rewarding than interviewing nursing-home residents. Over the course of my travels, I have interviewed hundreds of residents, and with few exceptions, I have found them to be both insightful and articulate. The questions on the accompanying form are the types I have asked numerous times—ones that get to the heart of the matter about nursing homes. Although skeptics may suggest that any resident who is interested in speaking with visitors or whom an administration is willing to volunteer for an interview is going to be a proponent of the home, be prepared for some big surprises during interviews with residents. I have frequently found that after a few minutes of conversation, residents will open up and be quite candid about their nursing-home experiences. Indeed, I have become uncomfortable at times upon hearing of parents abandoned by their children and facilities where staff is unresponsive and constantly angling for tips. This information is essential to the decision-making process, and residents are particularly qualified to discuss the subject of life in the nursing home. The last question frequently is the most revealing. While some residents may be reluctant to criticize, almost all are willing to suggest what needs to be done to improve life at the home.

Always remember that the nursing-home residents have an absolute right to their privacy; therefore, under no circumstances should you be questioning someone who is reluctant to speak with you or your team!

## RESIDENT QUESTIONNAIRE—PRELIMINARY VISIT

I. Background Information
   a. How long have you lived at this home?
   b. Why did you move into this nursing home?

II. Resident Issues
   a. What do you like about the home?
   b. What do you dislike about the home?
   c. How is the food?
   d. Are the nurses responsive to your needs?
   e. Does the staff try to help you when necessary?
   f. Is the activities program interesting and stimulating?
   g. Are you satisfied with the housekeeping here?
   h. How would you characterize the other residents of the nursing home? Are they nice? Friendly? Kind? Considerate? Boring? Nasty? Withdrawn? Argumentative?

i. What do the residents do to help new residents adjust to life in the nursing home?
j. What were your problems in making the transition to life in the home?
k. If you could change two things here, what would they be?

## Observations During the Visit

On the first visit and tour, it is impossible to do and see everything. However, during the course of the visit, it is imperative that the team makes some careful observations about the environment of the home, the condition of the residents, and the behavior of the staff vis-à-vis the residents. In the next several sections, I shall describe areas to address during the tour.

### The Smell Test

Nursing homes should not smell of urine. If they do, a red flag should go up, because that means the home is not active enough in dealing with continence problems. When there are odor problems, it frequently means also that the home is understaffed in nursing or housekeeping and the smell has permeated the drapes, rugs, and sometimes the furniture. While the olfactory senses may fatigue after a while, the reality of staffing problems does not go away. So if a home fails the smell test, the problem may be serious. Finally, do not be deceived by floral fragrances introduced into the air circulation systems; they merely mask the stench of urine and the true situation of the home.

### Cleanliness

During the tour and the visits to patients' rooms, observe how well housekeeping is taking care of the public hallways and the patient-care areas. Questions to be answered: Are bathrooms clean? Are floors and walls clean?

A good acid test is to check the dining room an hour or so after a meal. Has it been cleaned up? Is the floor free of food? Look carefully at the tables to see whether there is any food encrustation.

If there are housekeeping problems, note them and ask the administrator why they exist.

## Observe the Residents

During the course of your visit, you will have numerous opportunities to observe residents. Begin by looking at their clothes. Are the residents dressed properly for the weather? Are their clothes neat, clean, and in good repair? Are residents properly dressed for the time of day? Is their hair well combed? Does it appear clean?

When you shake hands with a resident, observe the state of his or her fingernails. Are they clean and a reasonable length? Look at the person's eyes. Are they free of crusts?

Look for signs of restraints, such as cloth straps on the beds and on wheelchairs. If you see a number of these, ask the nursing director about the home's policy on restraints.

## Observe the Staff

As you tour the facility, observe the activity of the staff, particularly in the nursing unit. Are the nurses and aides working with the residents or are they busy at the nursing station writing in charts? What appears to be the relationship between the nurses and the residents? In some homes that I have visited, there is a clear sense of mutual respect and camaraderie between these two groups. In others, unfortunately, the staff act as jailers and the residents behave like prisoners. A nursing home *must* be a place of dignity for the elderly, and the role of the staff is to serve the needs of the elderly in an efficient and effective manner. As you look around, try to collect evidence that can demonstrate how well the staff are doing their job at the home.

## Analyzing the Information

Although the process outlined can be exhausting, it is absolutely the best way to gather the data necessary to make a reasoned decision. There are no shortcuts. The next step is analysis of the material.

### Threshold Question

The first question that must be answered by all who are part of this decision: Based on what you have observed, are you comfortable with the reality of a nursing home for the prospective resident? Are there alternatives other than nursing homes that should be explored? A related question may be: Are there other nursing homes that should receive a preliminary visit?

### Tearing and Comparing

Finally it is time for all members of the team to compare notes about all the homes visited. It is best to prepare a simple summary chart that lists the strengths and weaknesses of the various homes visited and some preliminary conclusions about the apparent quality of care and quality of life offered to residents at each home. This chart can be used as the basis for the family discussion about the best solution. Obviously, nothing should be held back in this discussion, which should result in the selection of one or more homes for a second round of visits.

The process I have outlined is likely to end with the elimination of one or more homes so that perhaps one or more choices remain. Assuming agreement can be reached on one or two choices, and then it's time to prepare for the second round.

In Appendix 1 I have also included the Nursing-Home Checklist suggested by the center for nursing-home visits by the Medicare Nursing Home Compare website. It is a quite useful additional tool.

*No final decision should be made until after the second visit—the subject of the next chapter!*

# CHAPTER 12

# The Crucial Second Look

IMPORTANT NOTE: *If you follow just one of the many recommendations in this book, select this one: make a second visit to any nursing home or other long-term-care facility that is under serious consideration for yourself or a loved one!*

The goals of the second visit are to validate initial impressions, clarify the Medicare/Medicaid deficiency status of the nursing home, follow up on issues that may have come to mind after the first visit, and clarify the nature of any arrangements that need to be made prior to admission.

The reason the second visit turns out to be so important is simple: there is relatively little anxiety with the second trip because the people and the places are familiar. Nonetheless, as with the first set of interviews, the key to a successful visit is preparation. In this chapter, I discuss the strategy for being prepared and then suggest further issues to discuss with various staff members and residents of the home.

## Being Prepared: Two Steps

### Google and Bing the Home, Its Owners, and Its Parent Company

Thanks to Google, Bing, and the magic of the Internet we can get a great deal of information about organizations and people relatively quickly. Articles on the Internet, typically from local newspapers, can be useful. Such articles may be good stories about a facility and its programs or exposés. Regardless it is the simplest and fastest way of potentially doing homework.

### Do a Second Review of the Home's Most Recent Medicare Survey

This too can be done with the online documents readily available on the Internet. This review may bring up some questions that were not answered on the initial visit and the second go-around presents an opportunity for clarification. On the second visit, you may also wish to ask how things have improved since the surveyors wrote their public report.

For example, if staffing is below the state average and the home has received one or two stars in that area, you would want to know whether that is still the case. Do not settle for excuses such as the "surveyors never like us." While these surveys are not perfect, that are still the best available information!

## Obtaining Recommendations

The next action is to obtain references about the nursing home from people who have experienced its services. There are two problems connected with this: First, you need to get the names of people who have had dealings with the home; this may be simple or it may require some ingenuity. It is simple when the home and you are part of the same community and you or members of your family or friends know current or former residents. However, the problem of obtaining names is more complex when you are a stranger, although several options exist. Start with the home's social workers, and ask them whether they can provide the names of people who are involved with the home's activities and could serve as references. If that doesn't work, ask members of the local clergy if they know of any people in the community whom you could call for references. Another option is to call the local hospital and ask its social worker or discharge planner for names of potential reference givers. The hospital staff might also be able to provide the names of physicians who have patients at the home. Finally, if all else fails, contact the residents you met on the preliminary visit and ask them for names of several people whom you can call. However, since privacy is a great concern, don't expect 100 percent cooperation across the board.

Once you have established your calling list, it is best to speak (either face-to-face or on the phone) with each person and gather the information suggested on the basic Reference Form—Residents and Families, which accompanies this chapter. This form merely identifies the person who is giving the reference and suggests several questions geared toward opening the discussion about the home.

Next, there are specific questions about nursing, therapies, activities, administration, social services, food, and environment/sanitation. Each of these questions is designed to probe the experiences of the reference provider. It helps to ask the provider to identify specific examples, because by asking for these in addition to conclusions, you are in a better position to evaluate the weight you wish to assign to the reference. Finally, ask the reference giver if it is acceptable to call again if other questions come to mind. In some cases, another member of the decision group or perhaps the potential resident may wish to make the follow-up call.

## REFERENCE FORM—RESIDENTS AND FAMILIES

Date_______________
Reference's Name____________
Phone #____________

QUESTIONS

1. What is the nature of your contact with the nursing home?
2. Why did you (or your family) select this home?
3. Did you consider other homes in the area? Which ones? Why were they rejected?
4. How long have you [or your family member] resided in the home?
5. What type of care are you receiving (skilled or custodial)?
6. What has been your experience with the home?

7. Could you provide specific examples of positive and negative experiences you have had with the care at the home?
8. Is the nursing staff competent? Responsive? Any examples?
9. Do you feel that the activities program is sufficiently interesting and stimulating? Can you provide examples?
10. Has the therapy program (physical therapy, occupational therapy, art therapy, music therapy) proved to be interesting, stimulating, and/or helpful? Can you provide examples?
11. Is the administration responsive when you have problems? Can you provide examples?
12. Has the social-services department been helpful or not? Can you provide specific examples?
13. How is the food at the nursing home?
14. How is the general environment of the place? Is it clean and free of odors? Is it homelike or institutional? Is it a cheerful place?

CLOSING QUESTION

15. May I or a member of my family call you again if we have some additional questions?

Reference Taker ______________________________________________

## Recommendations from Care Providers

Present and even former providers of care at the nursing home can be an invaluable source of information about what goes on at the facility. There are two problems likely to be encountered in securing these recommendations. First, it frequently is difficult to identify the caregivers unless you are in a small community. Second, once you have identified some potential reference givers, it often is difficult to elicit candid opinions. In this section are some suggestions about dealing with these problems, and the Reference Form—Caregivers (at the end of this section) offers some questions that may overcome the natural reticence of these people to discuss their present or former organization.

Handling the first of these problems—that is, identifying knowledgeable caregivers—is primarily a matter of persistence. By doggedly calling a number of people, you undoubtedly will be able to identify several physicians, nurses, and therapists who have worked closely with the nursing home. Several starting points might be a family physician or friends who work in the local hospital as social workers, nurses, or therapists. Even if you do not know anyone in the community, you could stop by or call the local hospital and ask people in the social-services department for suggestions. Another contact is the local Council on the Elderly (or whatever name it uses). Stop by their offices, and ask the staff to help you identify potential sources of references. If you are living in a large city, local clergy may be helpful, as well as politicians, who make their living by knowing what is happening in their communities. In smaller towns, selectmen and other officials may be able to point you in the proper direction.

When you have identified several potential contacts, the next challenge is to get in touch with them and establish enough rapport so they will provide you with the answers you are seeking. Again, making contact is a matter of persistence. Begin by calling at the person's office, and if you cannot connect at the time, leave a message and a phone number. If you do not have a response within a day or two, make a second call and a third one if necessary. Consider telephoning early in the morning (before eight) or later in the afternoon (after five); often those are the best times to catch busy people. If all else fails, and the reference promises to be a crucial one, consider calling the person at home in the evening. While most of us do not wish to be disturbed then, remember that the stakes in this situation are very high and the decision you make has profound implications for everyone.

Once you have made contact, I suggest you spend a minute outlining your situation so that the person can have a frame of reference for his or her response. On the Reference Form—Care Providers is an outline of information you might want to provide prior to the questions. Next, a series of semi-open-ended questions may help the caregiver to focus his or her experiences in the nursing home as well as his or her analysis of the quality of care and quality of life at the home. Then I suggest you ask two closing questions, both of which request the reference provider to stand in your shoes and make a judgment about the home in terms of your needs. Obviously, the person at the other end of the phone does not have the total information about the potential resident, but these two questions do provide an opportunity for him or her to think about the home and your situation in a concrete manner.

A response to the last question that asks for suggestions about other homes may be particularly significant. For example, it would not be surprising if a present or former staff member would in his or her reluctance to talk to a stranger about the home give out a mixed message of praise for the home but a suggestion that you look at other places. Such a suggestion should be viewed as an indicator that the home has problems that should be investigated.

## REFERENCE FORM—CARE PROVIDERS

Date____________
Reference's Name______________________
Phone # ______________________

I. ***Rapport Building*** [It is suggested that you begin the conversation by describing the condition of the potential resident.]

***Suggested opening*** "Dr./Mr./Ms-________________________, I am sorry to bother you but I have a problem that you <u>may be able</u> to help me with. Your name was suggested to me by ______________ because of your association and experience with the ______________nursing home.

***Condition of potential resident***

a. My family is presently looking for a nursing home for my mother, who is __________years old.
b. She needs (total/some/no) assistance with the following activities of daily living: eating/bathing/toileting/transferring/dressing.
c. Her medical diagnosis is:

QUESTIONS

1. What type of involvement have you had with the nursing home?
2. What is your impression of the quality of care provided at the home?
3. Can you provide examples of good or poor care given at the home?
4. What is your impression of the quality of life at the home for residents? Can you provide examples of good or poor aspects?

CLOSING QUESTIONS

5. From what I have told you about my mother, do you think the _______ nursing home would be a good placement?
6. Could you suggest any other nursing homes in the area that would be a better place for my mother?

Reference Taker ____________________________________________

## Using the Data from the References

The data from the references will be all negative, all positive, or mixed. Consistently negative reviews should cause you to contemplate eliminating this home from your list. If competent, experienced witnesses all have found the home wanting, there is a high probability that you would also be dissatisfied with it. While it is possible that the reference givers are biased and do not see the strengths of the home, or perhaps they have a vendetta against the home, the more likely explanation is that the home is of poor quality. Although it is difficult to go back to square one, it probably is a wiser course of action than settling for an inadequate facility and the hassles that you will encounter in trying to make such a home responsive to your needs.

Reviews that are all positive or mixed provide guidance for the second site visit. In both instances, the primary value of the reference check will be to identify areas for further inquiry on your second visit. For example, if several people point up problems with a boring and pedestrian activities program, you may want to spend extra time looking into that. On the other hand, if everyone raves about the food, it probably is not worth making an effort to examine the food services at the home.

Regardless of the findings, this second visit is absolutely necessary. The next section covers that visit, proposing what areas need exploration and including a list of suggested questions.

## The Second Visit and New Questions

The second visit to a nursing home will likely be more useful than the first one. The anxiety will be significantly diminished because you will be familiar with the home and its people. Also, you will be a more experienced and sophisticated visitor than on your first visit. But just as with the first visit, it will be necessary to call the administrator (or in some cases the admitting office) to arrange the interviews and tour.

This second visit provides the opportunity to probe areas of concern and clarify ambiguities about care at the home. From the survey documents that you have read, some questions should already be in mind (better yet, written down). In addition, you should consider asking the questions that appear on the accompanying Second-Visit Questionnaire. Most of these are the same or similar to questions that trained interviewers ask when they visit the nursing home. In many instances, the proper answers are obvious, and in all instances, the answers will clarify how the nursing home is treating residents and how it is likely to treat a new resident.

### SECOND-VISIT QUESTIONNAIRE

A. Questions for Residents
   1. How long have you lived in this nursing home? Why are you here?
   2. What responsibilities do you have in living here? How were you informed about these responsibilities?
   3. If there are changes in services or costs, does someone explain these?

4. To what extent has your doctor talked to you about your health and your treatment?
    a. Do you know that you can refuse treatment or medication?
5. Have you or has anyone you know at the nursing home ever refused treatment or medication? If yes, what happened to you or to them?
7. Are the staff and administration responsive to complaints? To whom can you complain?
8. Does the nursing home hold any money that belongs to you? How easy or difficult is it for you to obtain that money?
9. Has anything been stolen from you while at the nursing home? What did the staff or administration do about it?
10. Have you ever been restrained? If yes, why were you restrained? Do you know why you were restrained?
11. Do you feel safe in this facility?
12. What degree of privacy and respect do you receive?
13. Can you have visits and phone calls from anyone? Is there adequate privacy in the nursing home?
14. What are your favorite activities at the home?
15. Is participation optional or required?
16. Do you have any trouble getting to off-campus activities?
17. Do you know of any resident who was transferred out of the home? Why was he or she transferred? To your knowledge, was the transfer discussed with the resident and his or her family before the move?
18. How often does your personal physician visit? Is it often enough? If you want to see your doctor, is it easily arranged?
19. If you have bowel or bladder problems, what type of help do you get from the staff?
20. If you need help getting to the toilet, how long do you need to wait to be taken there?
21. Do residents generally feel that people taking care of them know what they are doing? If no, please explain.
22. How long do you usually wait for help when you put your call light on?

23. What assistance do you need in the following areas, and if you do need assistance, who provides it: bathing, dressing, eating, getting into and out of bed, getting in and out of a wheelchair, going to the toilet?
24. Do you feel that the assistance provided to you is done in an appropriate manner? For example, if you need help getting into or out of bed, do you feel safe when being helped?
25. If you have trouble sleeping, can you get assistance? What type of assistance?
26. Is your cane, crutch, or walker comfortable for you to use?
27. Do you always receive your medications on time? Does the nurse stay with you as you take your medications?
28. How is the food? Is it tasty? Are the portions sufficient? How do you get food outside of regular mealtimes?
29. How often does someone from dietary visit you to ask about your opinions on the food service?
30. Do you receive any kind of therapy here, such as physical therapy, occupational therapy, or speech therapy? If yes, why do you receive the therapy? How long have you received the therapy? Where do you receive the therapy? What happens if the therapist is absent?
31. Is your room kept clean? What about the rest of the nursing home?
32. If you could make some changes around the nursing home, what would they be?

B. Questions for Nurses

1. What is the standard procedure if a resident claims that something was stolen from him or her?
2. How do you get medical information and orders on a new resident?
3. How often do physicians normally visit residents in the home?
4. Who are the physicians with the most residents in the home? How much time do they spend with a resident on a typical visit?

5. How do you choose what clothing each of your residents wears each day? What do you do if a resident insists on wearing dirty or mismatched clothes?
   What is the schedule for bathing residents and washing hair?
6. Does the nursing home have a special bowel- and bladder-training program?
7. Do you think that there is enough help in this nursing home? If no, why not?
9. What do you do about residents who are having trouble sleeping?
10. How many residents receive physical therapy, occupational therapy, or speech therapy?

C. Questions for Administration
   1. How do residents learn what is expected of them?
   2. How do residents learn of changes in the nursing home's procedures or charges?
   3. Is the nursing home participating in any research projects that directly or indirectly involve residents? If yes, what are these projects? How many residents are involved? What arrangements are made to secure their informed consent?
   4. What is the facility's policy concerning restraints? Do you make a distinction between safety devices and restraints? If so, what is the policy for safety devices?
   5. Who trains staff in use of restraints?
   6. What type of activities goes on during the evening hours and on weekends?
   7. Who is notified if a resident is injured?
   8. What is the nursing home's policy on notifying a relative or responsible other party if a resident's condition changes?
   9. What is the nursing home's policy regarding physician visits?
   10. Have any physicians on your medical staff been disciplined? If yes, why?

11. Who provides therapy to the home's residents?
12. How many people were transferred out of this nursing home to another nursing home within the past year? What were the circumstances of the transfer?

D. Questions for Social-Services Staff
   1. How are roommate assignments made? What is the process for changing roommates or room assignments? To what extent does cost enter into the decision about room assignment?
   2. What is done to maintain resident dignity?
   3. How is transportation arranged for off-campus activities?
   4. Do residents participate in their plans for care?
   5. How often does social services meet with a resident's family?
   6. How often does social services meet with nursing?
   7. How frequently do residents get out of the facility for activities?

## Areas for Additional Observation

During the course of this second visit, it is imperative to observe carefully what is happening at the nursing home. Here are areas for particular attention:

1. Do you see any examples of obviously inappropriate roommate situations, such as an alert resident rooming with a noisy and confused person?
2. Are the interactions between the staff and residents free of harassment, threats, and humiliation?
3. Are there areas for residents to be alone or meet in private with friends and relatives?
4. Are residents appropriately dressed for the time of day and the weather?
5. Do resident rooms appear to be deinstitutionalized with some personal furniture or other belongings?

6. Is there enough space to store clothing?
7. Are residents clean and free of odors? Is there crusting around their eyelids? Are eyeglasses properly fitted and clean? Are there dried-food particles or drool around the mouth? Does hair appear to be clean and combed or brushed? Are nails clean and of the appropriate length?
8. If you see a resident in need of assistance, is that resident being assisted? Is it being done in a safe and competent manner? Does the staff appear to be minimizing pain and discomfort while assisting the resident?
9. Does the facility have grab bars in all the corridors? Are the resident rooms functional? Do the bathrooms have grab bars around the toilets?
10. Observe—better yet, eat a meal in—the residents' dining hall. Observe whether there is enough time for the meal. Is assistance provided to those people who need it? Are any adaptive eating devices being used? Are residents' clothes being protected? Is there adequate space in the dining room and at the table?
11. Ask to see sample menus that cover a week or more.
12. Ask for a tour of the kitchen. Look for rust on shelves, dripping or spillage on shelves or floors, or dirty food preparation equipment.
13. Ask for a tour of the therapy area. Does the equipment appear to be clean and in good working order?
14. Finally, observe the general condition of the home. Is the paint chipped? Are the public spaces clean and free of odors?

## Decisions and Deals

Now comes the hardest part of the process: making a decision and finalizing the deal. The decision amounts to this:

After comparing several nursing homes, which one will provide the best quality of care and quality of life for the resident? The data collected from the various references and the two visits will most often point in one direction.

By conducting the type of in-depth research and analysis suggested in this book, family members will be able to distance themselves from the superficial considerations that frequently cause people to choose a facility that looks good initially but turns out later to be problematic. You can avoid this if you are a prudent buyer and make your decision on the basis of substance, not superficial amenities.

Once the selection is made, it is absolutely imperative to obtain a copy of the contract that you will be expected to sign with the nursing home. (Appendix 3 has a sample contract.) Do not sign this contract without carefully reviewing and, if appropriate, questioning each word and sentence in it. You may want to hire an attorney to read the contract and negotiate any changes—the time to make changes is *before* admission. After admission, there is practically no leverage for making a contract change.

If you have a major medical problem, going to the Mayo Clinic in Rochester, Minnesota, may make a great deal of sense. But if you need a nursing home, you do not have to go to a medical mecca, since there may be an excellent facility in your community or only a short ride away. In the next chapter, I will focus on the elements of an excellent nursing home and share my experiences of visiting some of the nation's best facilities.

# CHAPTER 13

# Finding a First-Class Nursing Home: The Elements of Excellence

## Introduction

Almost three decades ago, I began my research on nursing homes by examining those elements that make a nursing home an outstanding place as well as a searching for the *best* nursing homes in America. I thought that if I could find, analyze, and describe the *best*, it could become the model for the nation's other homes.

I was wrong! Despite my expectations and my visit to scores of nursing homes in dozens of states, later expanded to other countries, I did not find the one *best* home. Instead, I encountered numerous excellent homes. These homes were in dozens of communities from Portland, Oregon, to Portland, Maine, Southern California to southern Florida, and myriad points in between. Indeed, I doubt that there even is a best home; rather, what exists are many homes with excellent and unusual programs and staff, but no one home has it all. And the reality is, as noted earlier, that it does not matter. Any decision about placing a family member in a nursing facility is constrained by location and logistics. This chapter summarizes the essence of this book by identifying nine elements of an excellent nursing home and presenting some supporting examples.

## Element 1: Mission

It is absolutely obvious to me that first-class nursing homes are those where there is a clear mission related to some philosophical, religious, or patriotic commitment. Examples might include government-owned nursing homes for veterans, homes developed and affiliated with religious organizations, and homes associated with fraternal organizations. Typically such a home has a well-articulated philosophy that often serves as a constant reminder to staff, residents, family, and visitors what the nursing home is all about. Similarly a well-articulated mission serves as a touchstone for managerial and board leadership.

Perhaps the best philosophy is the one that no one should be in a nursing home unless it is absolutely necessary. It is also one that is not attempting to "sell" the nursing home but rather to assist people in the search for programmatic alternatives to nursing-home care. Sometimes a *mission commitment* comes out in less noticeable ways, that is, action, not words!

For example, I attended the meeting of the board of directors' executive committee of a not-for-profit nursing home where the subject was recruitment of an activities staff person for the Alzheimer's unit. The recommendation presented to the committee was to hire a part-time activities person for the unit. This was challenged by one board member, who argued that, despite the home's projected deficit, it was in the best interests of the unit's residents to have a full-time activities person. Finally, he noted, "So we are $500,000 in the hole; we'll be another $40,000 deeper." His recommendation was accepted.

## Element 2: Economic Orientation

While this is a country committed to free-enterprise capitalism, and the profit motive may give us better disposable diapers or Internet giants, it does not work so well in the area of long-term care for the elderly.

To put it bluntly, you are more likely to get the most substantive value for your nursing-home dollars in a government-owned facility or a not-for-profit home owned by an organization rooted in a religious or charitable trust. As noted earlier in this book, government and not-for-profit homes, that are not attempting to earn an income for investors, inevitably have higher staffing ratios and active volunteer programs (which add staff without cost) and frequently operate at a deficit, which is covered through active fund-raising programs or endowments.

An unfortunate reality is that in many parts of the country, Medicaid does not allow a nursing home to be profitable unless the home cuts corners and provides staff exactly at state minimum levels. In those states, residents of homes that cater to Medicaid beneficiaries will have limited services, and both the quality-of-life activities and the quality of care will be barely adequate, at best.

Since money appears to be a crucial factor in whether or not one can get into a nursing home, it is frequently difficult to have the option of choosing between "sizzle" and "steak" in nursing homes. Careful applicants sometimes can get both. The trick is simple: do not be hoodwinked by plush lobbies, grand pianos, and antique reproduction furniture. These facilities frequently are targeting their marketing to guilt-ridden children—"Mom, look at this beautiful hotel you will be in." On the other hand, the well-staffed, well-organized place may choose to make its investment in staff and programs, not in assuaging the children's guilt.

## Element 3: Governance

An active governing board makes a big difference. While the not-for-profits and many government homes have boards, there is nothing to preclude a privately owned nursing home from establishing, at a minimum, an advisory board. Such boards, governing or advisory, meet periodically to monitor and evaluate the functioning of the institution. A good board that is knowledgeable and concerned about the nursing home and does not have a personal financial stake in the facility brings a measure of oversight and ideas that can be very useful.

While I am clearly a proponent of not-for-profit homes, I also believe that a dedicated board (or owners) in the for-profit sector can provide excellent oversight. During my twenty-one years on the board of Extendicare, I was pleased with how carefully our board dealt with the quality and safety issues at our hundreds of homes and how professionally our executives responded to our policy concerns. For example, in 2003 a tragic fire killed eight residents and seriously injured sixteen others in a Tennessee nursing home that failed to have sprinklers. Subsequent to that incident, the then CEO Mel Rhinelander proposed spending over $10 million to add sprinklers to all the Extendicare homes that were not sprinkled. The board immediately approved and agreed with the CEO's expedited schedule to implement the project despite the fact that sprinklers were not a requirement in many states where the company operated, nor was the $10 million a cost that Medicare, Medicaid, or any state would reimburs. Incidentally Extendicare no longer owns or operates any facilities in the United States; it is now a "pure-play Canadian senior care and service provider."

## Element 4: Medical Staff

Several recent research studies have demonstrated what most people intuitively know, that is, a medical staff who spends more than a token amount of time in a nursing home has positive results for the residents. These results include fewer hospitalizations and less readmissions to hospitals after any incidents. Primarily what are necessary are a medical staff as well as nurse-practitioners and appropriate facility infrastructure. For example, at the Miami Jewish Health System, there is an ambulatory health clinic that offers numerous clinical services including orthopedic, radiology, and various consultative services.

## Element 5: Nursing

With regard to nurses, there are several concerns. First, does the home have enough? The answer to this question will be found in the data from "Nursing Home Compare." As noted earlier what is not so readily available is data on the use of agency/pool nurses. Homes will little or no agency/pool nurses are usually the most desired facilities.

Another significant issue is whether the home has recruited people with the appropriate level of experience and maturity to handle the jobs. For example, at one privately owned home in Texas, I met the evening supervisor, an RN who held a master's degree and also was a recently retired colonel from the nurse corps of the US Army. Knowing that such an experienced and qualified person is on duty in the evening builds confidence in an institution. All the excellent homes were filled with people who were interested and committed to the elderly and who frequently had advanced training in a range of gerontological specialties.

## Element 6: Therapeutic Services

Many nursing homes either provide or arrange for the basic physical, occupational, and speech therapy services described earlier. Excellence exists when a home provides these services with well-trained therapists and aides and also when these services are easily accessible to the residents—that is, they are essentially part of the institution's routine program. Frankly, many homes only provide the therapeutic services on a contract basis if there is an additional private or Medicare payment for the services. Unfortunately, when this is the case, those who cannot afford the services will experience a slow but steady loss of strength and functioning as a result.

An excellent home also provides a broad range of additional therapeutic services that deal with the physical and emotional needs of the residents. Among these is social-service counseling for residents and their families, art therapy, gardening therapy, pet therapy, music therapy, and dance therapy. It should be reemphasized that there is a world of difference between the activities of art therapy and the typical painting activity prevalent in many homes. Painting or sculpting may be good *therapy*, but at some homes it is part of a program to diagnose and treat a range of emotional programs. In those homes these therapists are truly part of the clinical-care team whose observations and analyses are used by social workers, nurses, and physicians to develop and modify treatment plans.

In addition to having the right staff, a good therapy program needs facilities and equipment as well as comfortable space. Even a well-organized garden-therapy program needs more than just a plot of earth. For example, at several homes I've observed raised garden boxes, which allow residents to maneuver their wheelchairs close enough so they could reach in and do their work.

Overall, the therapeutic programs provide a bulwark against emotional and physical deterioration. The truly excellent homes *do* provide those services without a major concern about the costs.

## Element 7: Activities

All nursing homes have bingo, a game I have come to detest. Indeed, bingo is the central activity in many homes. In speaking with nursing-home staff about the game, I have been told many times that it is what the residents want. In my judgment, it is not what is wanted but what is given.

Even the excellent homes have bingo. But they also have a great deal more—they have action. For example, I've visited homes that take residents on weekly trips to local restaurants, shopping centers, zoos, and concerts. Other homes have arrangements with local summer camps whereby teenage volunteers simply talk with the residents a few times a week. Several other homes operate sheltered workshops for residents where they can participate in a range of supervised projects and earn spending money.

The key to the excellent facility is one that is interested in being a stimulating home for its residents, not merely a warehouse where the elderly wait to die.

## Element 8: Physical Facilities

The best nursing homes I visited were always well maintained, bright, and cheerful. Many homes have beauty parlors and barbershops, indoor and outdoor greenhouses, chapels, in-house cable-television systems, libraries, and snack bars and gift shops that sell a range of items from sugar-free candy to clothes.

In terms of design, there is a clear need for large and comfortable living-room-type spaces, both indoor and outdoor, where families can visit away from a resident's bedroom with a modicum of privacy.

In terms of the residents' own rooms, I was always impressed with the homes that encouraged residents to create their own private spaces with pictures, a piece of furniture from home, or a favorite bedcover. Since many residents wind up sharing a room, it was particularly interesting to see cleverly designed semiprivate rooms where beds in narrow, elongated rooms were placed essentially toe-to-toe so that each resident of a double room has access to a window.

## Element 9: Top-Level Managerial Sensitivity

Perhaps what most distinguishes the truly excellent facility from the fair or poor home is the sensitivity of top management to the needs of the elderly and the translation of that sensitivity into action.

The best example of this comes from an experience I had in a small town in England, where I was visiting a two-hundred-bed nursing home built on the edge of a new development. Within weeks of the home's opening, it filled to capacity, and the management experienced the problem of old men wandering away in the early evening hours. Eventually they were all located in the pubs in their old neighborhoods, and the home's solution is a case study in sensitivity, responsiveness, and creativity. The nursing home established its own pub, which was opened to the neighborhood. Soon the home became the focal point for neighborhood gatherings, and the home's residents no longer had to be chased down throughout the town.

It is also important to find a nursing-home administrator who makes it his or her business to stay in touch with the residents and staff by walking around the home several times a week and keeping in contact with the families. Some go so far as to hold monthly family socials, which serve varying communication and support functions. Others interact by teaching classes for residents in current events and even leading religious services. The common denominator is simply that the administrator is not isolated from the most important people at the home: the residents!

Many homes now have photos or collages of residents posted on their doors. These memory boxes often contain photos and biographical material, invaluable information for the resident as well as the staff developing a sense of community and helping them better understand the resident.

Finally, the sensitive management is an advocate of residents' rights (Appendix 2). For such management staff, these rights are not merely federal or state legal requirements but rather a code that ensures the dignity of life for the elderly.

## A Final Word

As I travel around the country, I frequently ask members of large groups how many of them expect to spend the last few years of their lives in a nursing home. Usually no one raises a hand. When a brave soul does say that he or she expects it to happen, it usually is because that person has a loved one in a good nursing home. A good or better yet an excellent home is not a place to fear but rather a place to live. I will have done my job if this book helps you move closer to finding that excellent home.

# Appendices

Appendix 1 Nursing-Home Checklist · · · 175

Appendix 2 Residents' Rights and Protections · · · 183

Appendix 3 Example of a Long-Term-Care Contract · · · 191

Appendix 4 Fact Sheet on Nursing-Home Agreements Reprinted With Permission from California Advocates for Nursing Home Reform · · · 219

# APPENDIX 1

## Nursing-Home Checklist

As an alternative to the more extensive questionnaires that I have developed in this book, I am including in this appendix a checklist or a set of questions that has been prepared by the Centers for Medicare & Medicaid Services. The actual form they use has spaces for "YES," "NO," and "Notes" for each question. This form is available on Nursing Home Compare website: Medicare.gov/nursinghomecompare.

### Nursing home checklist

Name of nursing home: ______________________________

Address: ______________________________

Phone number: ______________________________

Date of visit: ______________________________

Basic information

Is the nursing home Medicare certified?

Is the nursing home Medicaid certified?

Does the nursing home have the level of care I need?

Does the nursing home have a bed available?

Does the nursing home offer specialized services, like a special care unit for a resident with dementia, ventilator care, or rehabilitation services?

Is the nursing home located close enough for friends and family to visit?

Resident appearance

Are the residents clean, well groomed, and appropriately dressed for the season or time of day?

Nursing home living spaces

Is the nursing home free from overwhelming unpleasant odors?

Does the nursing home appear clean and well kept?

Is the temperature in the nursing home comfortable for residents?

Does the nursing home have good lighting?

Are the noise levels in the dining room and other common areas comfortable?

Is smoking allowed? If so, is it restricted to certain areas of the nursing home?

Is the furniture sturdy, yet comfortable and attractive?

Staff

Does the relationship between the staff and residents appear to be warm, polite, and respectful?

Does the staff wear nametags?

Does the staff knock on the door before entering a resident's room? Do they refer to residents by name?

Does the nursing home offer a training and continuing education program for all staff?

Does the nursing home check to make sure they don't hire staff members who have been found guilty of abuse, neglect or mistreatment of residents; or have a finding of abuse, neglect, or mistreatment of residents in the state nurse aid registry?

Is there a licensed nursing staff 24 hours a day, including a Registered Nurse (RN) present at least 8 hours per day, 7 days a week?

Will a team of nurses and Certified Nursing Assistants (CNAs) work with me to meet my needs?

Do CNAs help plan the care of residents?

Is there a person on staff that will be assigned to meet my social service needs?

Will the staff call my doctor for me if I have a medical need?

Has there been a turnover in administration staff, like the administrator or director of nurses, in the past year?

Residents' rooms

Can residents have personal belongings and furniture in their rooms?

Does each resident have storage space (closet and drawers) in his or her room?

Does each resident have a window in his or her bedroom?

Do residents have access to a personal phone and television?

Do residents have a choice of roommates?

Are there policies and procedures to protect residents' possessions, including lockable cabinets and closets?

Hallway, stairs, lounges, & bathrooms

Are exits clearly marked?

Are there quiet areas where residents can visit with friends and family?

Does the nursing home have smoke detectors and sprinklers?

Are all common areas, resident rooms, and doorways designed for wheelchair use?

Are handrails and grab bars appropriately placed in the hallways and bathrooms?

Menus & food

Do residents have a choice of food items at each meal? (Ask if your favorite foods are served.)

Can the nursing home provide for special dietary needs (like low-salt or no-sugar-added diets)?

Are nutritious snacks available upon request?

Does the staff help residents eat and drink at mealtimes if help is needed?

Activities

Can residents, including those who are unable to leave their rooms, choose to take part in a variety of activities?

Do residents help plan or choose activities that are available?

Does the nursing home have outdoor areas for resident use? Is the staff available to help residents go outside?

Does the nursing home have an active volunteer program?

Safety & care

Does the nursing home have an emergency evacuation plan and hold regular fire drills (bed-bound residents included)?

Do residents get preventive care, like a yearly flu shot, to help keep them healthy? Does the facility help arrange hearing screenings or vision tests?

Can residents still see their personal doctors? Does the facility help arrange transportation for this purpose?

How often are charts reviewed by a doctor?

Does the nursing home have an arrangement with a nearby hospital for emergencies?

Are care plan meetings held with residents and family members at times that are convenient and flexible whenever possible?

Has the nursing home corrected all deficiencies (failure to meet one or more state or federal requirements) on its last state inspection report?

Does the nursing home have specific policies and procedures related to the care of individuals with dementia? If so, does the policy include the use of non-medication based approaches to care as a first attempt to respond to behavioral symptoms, which are often a means of communication, for patients living with dementia?

What percentage of resident's who have a diagnosis of dementia are currently being prescribed an antipsychotic medication?

What's the nursing home's current rate of antipsychotic medication use?

Does the nursing home participate in any efforts related to reducing the use of antipsychotic medication in nursing homes? (These include National Partnership to Improve Dementia Care, National Nursing Home Quality Care Collaborative, and Advancing Excellence in America's Nursing Homes Campaign.)

Go to a resident council or family council meeting

While you're visiting the nursing home, ask a member of the resident council if you can attend a resident council or family council meeting. These councils are usually organized and managed by the residents or the residents' families to address concerns and improve the quality of care and life for the resident.

If you're able to go to a meeting, ask a council member these questions and take notes:

- What improvements were made to the quality of life for residents in the last year?
- What are the plans for future improvements?

- How has the nursing home responded to recommendations for improvement?
- Who does the council report to?
- How does membership on the council work?
- Who sets the agendas for meetings?
- How are decisions made (for example, by voting, consensus, or one person makes them)?

Visit again

It's a good idea to visit the nursing home a second time. It's best to visit a nursing home on a different day of the week and at a different time of day than your initial visit. Staffing can be different at different times of the day and on weekends.

Notes on second visit:

# APPENDIX 2

## Residents' Rights and Protections

(This document is from the Center for Medicare & Medicaid Services.)

### Your Rights and Protections as a Nursing Home Resident

#### What are my rights in a nursing home?

As a nursing home resident, you have certain rights and protections under Federal and state law that help ensure you get the care and services you need. You have the right to be informed, make your own decisions, and have your personal information kept private.

The nursing home must tell you about these rights and explain them in writing in a language you understand. They must also explain in writing how you should act and what you're responsible for while you're in the nursing home. This must be done before or at the time you're admitted, as well as during your stay. You must acknowledge in writing that you got this information.

At a minimum, Federal law specifies that nursing homes must protect and promote the following rights of each resident. You have the right to:

**Be Treated with Respect**: You have the right to be treated with dignity and respect, as well as make your own schedule and participate in the activities you choose. You have the right to decide when you go to bed, rise in the morning, and eat your meals.

**Participate in Activities:** You have the right to participate in an activities program designed to meet your needs and the needs of the other residents.

**Be Free from Discrimination:** Nursing homes don't have to accept all applicants, but they must comply with Civil Rights laws that say they can't discriminate based on race, color, national origin, disability, age, or religion.

The Department of Health and Human Services, Office for Civil Rights has more information. Visit http://www.hhs.gov/ocr.

**Be Free from Abuse and Neglect:** You have the right to be free from verbal, sexual, physical, and mental abuse. Nursing homes can't keep you apart from everyone else against your will. If you feel you have been mistreated (abused) or the nursing home isn't meeting your needs (neglect), report this to the nursing home, your family, your local Long-Term Care Ombudsman, or State Survey Agency. The nursing home must investigate and report all suspected violations and any injuries of unknown origin within 5 working days of the incident to the proper authorities.

**Be Free from Restraints:** Nursing homes can't use any physical restraints (like side rails) or chemical restraints (like drugs) to discipline you for the staffs own convenience.

**Mak e Complaints:** You have the right to make a complaint to the staff of the nursing home, or any other person, without fear of punishment. The nursing home must address the issue promptly.

**Get Proper Medical Care:** You have the following rights regarding your medical care:

To be fully informed about your total health status in a language you understand.

To be fully informed about your medical condition, prescription and over-the-counter drugs, vitamins, and supplements.

To be involved in the choice of your doctor.

To participate in the decisions that affects your care.

To take part in developing your care plan. By law, nursing homes must develop a care plan for each resident. You have the right to take part in this process. Family members can also help with your care plan with your permission.

To access all your records and reports, including clinical records (medical records and reports) promptly (on weekdays). Your legal guardian has the right to look at all your medical records and make important decisions on your behalf.

To express any complaints (sometimes called "grievances") you have about your care or treatment.

To create advance directives (a health care proxy or power of attorney, a living will, after-death wishes) in accordance with State law.

To refuse to participate in experimental treatment.

**Have Your Representative Notified:** The nursing home must notify your doctor and, if known, your legal representative or an interested family member when the following occurs:

You're involved in an accident and are injured and/or need to see a doctor. Your physical, mental, or psychosocial status starts to get worse.

You have a life threatening condition.

You have medical complications.

Your treatment needs to change significantly.

The nursing home decides to transfer or discharge you from the nursing home.

**Get Information on Services and Fees:** You have the right to be told in writing about all nursing home services and fees (those that are charged and not charged to you) before you move into the nursing home and at any time when services and fees change. In addition:

The nursing home can't require a minimum entrance fee if your care is paid for by Medicare or Medicaid.

For people seeking admission to the nursing home, the nursing home must tell you (both orally and in writing) and also display written information about how to apply for and use Medicare and Medicaid benefits.

The nursing home must also provide information on how to get a refund if you paid for an item or service, but because of Medicare and Medicaid eligibility rules, it's now considered covered.

**Manage Your Money**: You have the right to manage your own money or to choose someone you trust to do this for you. In addition:

If you deposit your money with the nursing home or ask them to hold or account for your money, you must sign a written statement saying you want them to do this.

The nursing home must allow you access to your bank accounts, cash, and other financial records.

The nursing home must have a system that ensures full accounting for your funds and can't combine your funds with the nursing home's funds.

The nursing home must protect your funds from any loss by providing an acceptable protection, such as buying a surety bond.

If a resident with a fund dies, the nursing home must return the funds with a final accounting to the person or court handling the resident's estate within 30 days.

**Get Proper Privacy, Property, and Living Arrangements:** You have the following rights:

To keep and use your personal belongings and property as long as they don't interfere with the rights, health, or safety of others.

To have private visits.

To make and get private phone calls.

To have privacy in sending and getting mail and email.

To have the nursing home protect your property from theft.

To share a room with your spouse if you both live in the same nursing home (if you both agree to do so).

The nursing home has to notify you before your room or your roommate is changed and should take your preferences into account.

To review the nursing home's health and fire safety inspection results.

**Spend Time with Visitors:** You have the following rights:

To spend private time with visitors.

To have visitors at any time, as long as you wish to see them, as long as the visit does not interfere with the provision of care and privacy rights of other residents

To see any person who gives you help with your health, social, legal, or other services may at any time. This includes your doctor, a representative from the health department, and your Long-Term Care Ombudsman, among others.

**Get Social Services:** The nursing home must provide you with any needed social services, including the following:

Counseling.

Help solving problems with other residents.

Help in contacting legal and financial professionals. Discharge planning.

**Leave the Nursing Home:**

Leaving for visits: If your health allows, and your doctor agrees, you can spend time away from the nursing home visiting family or friends during the day or overnight, called a "leave of absence." Talk to the nursing home staff a few days ahead of time so the staff has time to prepare your medicines and write your instructions. Caution: If your nursing home care is covered by certain health insurance, you may not be able to leave for visits without losing your coverage.

Moving out: Living in a nursing home is your choice. You can choose to move to another place. However, the nursing home may have a policy that requires you to tell them before you plan to leave. If you don't, you may have to pay an extra fee.

**Have Protection Against Unfair Transferor Discharge:** You can't be sent to another nursing home, or made to leave the nursing home, unless any of the following are true:

It's necessary for the welfare, health, or safety of you or others.

Your health has improved to the point that nursing home care is no longer necessary. The nursing home hasn't been paid for services you got.

The nursing home closes.

You have the following rights:

You have the right to appeal a transfer or discharge to the State.

The nursing home can't make you leave if you're waiting to get Medicaid.

Except in emergencies, nursing homes must give a 3D-day written notice of their plan and reason to discharge or transfer you.

The nursing home has to safely and orderly transfer or discharge you and give you proper notice of bed-hold and/or readmission requirements.

**Form or Participate in Resident Groups:** You have a right to form or participate in a resident group to discuss issues and concerns about the nursing home's policies and operations. Most homes have such groups, often called "resident councils." The home must give you meeting space and must listen to and act upon grievances and recommendations of the group.

**Have Your Family and Friends Involved:** Family and friends can help make sure you get good quality care. They can visit and get to know the staff and the nursing home's rules. Family members and legal guardians may meet with the families of other residents and may participate in family councils, if one exists. Family members can help with your care plan with your permission. If a family member or friend is your legal guardian, he or she has the right to look at all medical records about you and make important decisions on your behalf.

# APPENDIX 3

## Example of a Long-Term-Care Contract

LONG TERM CARE RESIDENT ADMISSION AGREEMENT

RESIDENT ADMISSION AGREEMENT for:

Resident: (print full name)

Responsible Party: (print full name)

Home address:

Home phone:

Work phone:

Relationship to Resident:

Rev 05/13

## Article I. Definitions

1.1. In order to make this Agreement of Admission ("Agreement") more easily understandable, all second person pronouns (such as "you", "your", "yours", etc.) refer to the Resident. All first person pronouns (such as "we", "us", "our", "ours", etc.), as well as the terms "the House" and "Facility," refer to ABC NURSING HOME.

1.2. As used in this Agreement, the term "Responsible Party" refers to the individual named in this Agreement as Responsible Party and as whose duties are more fully described in Article IV.

## Article II. Introduction and Mutual Promises

2.1. This Agreement is a legally binding contract between and among you, the Responsible Party and us. By signing this Agreement, you and the Responsible Party are legally bound by it. In consideration of the mutual promises, representations and warranties set forth in this Agreement, you, the Responsible Party and we agree as follows.

## Article III. Our Responsibilities

3.1. We will provide you with the items and services set forth in Exhibit "A" to this Agreement which are presently included in our daily rate.

3.2. If you are eligible for Medicaid, we will provide you with the items and services set forth in Exhibit "B" to this Agreement which are included in the Medicaid daily rate

3.3. If you request any item(s) or service(s) for which we will make an additional charge, we will notify you of the amount of the charge.

3.4. You and your Responsible Party agree and acknowledge that if you are not covered by Medicare or Medicaid, or if your insurer should decline coverage you will be billed directly for the services identified as being generally covered by Medicare or Medicaid in Exhibits "A" and "B" to this agreement.

________(Your initials or the Responsible Party's initials)

## Article IV. Your/Responsible Party Responsibilities

4.1. You shall timely pay all fees and charges due under this Agreement.

4.2. The Responsible Party shall ensure that all fees and charges due under this Agreement are timely paid from your income, assets and resources.

4.3. You and/or the Responsible Party shall provide such as you need or desire and remove them within seventy-two (72) hours after discharge; any such items not removed within ten (10) days after discharge will be donated to charity.

4.4. You and/or the Responsible Party shall provide your own spending money for your personal needs (the Medicaid program will allow Medicaid eligible residents to retain a sum of $ from their income for their personal needs).

4.5. You and/or the Responsible Party shall pay for the use of a telephone or cable television service in your room. We will bill you $_______monthly, plus long-distance toll fees for personal telephone service. Our charges for cable television service for your personal use is $______, for which we will bill you monthly.

I wish to have personal telephone service in my room._

Yes______No

_________(Your initials or the Responsible Party's initials)

I wish to have cable television service in my room._____

Yes______No

_________(Your initials or the Responsible Party's initials)

4.6. You and/or the Responsible Party shall pay ancillary service, hospital or other health care facility charges, including transportation charges, incurred when you utilize such services if they are not covered by Medicare, Medicaid or third-party insurance.

4.7. You and/or the Responsible Party shall pay all funeral and burial arrangements and related costs.

4.8. You and your Responsible Party shall notify the facility's social worker or finance office when your assets fall below the amount necessary to pay for six (6) months of care and ancillary services. As soon as you are eligible or entitled, you and the Responsible Party shall apply for and seek to establish eligibility and entitlement to receive benefits under the Medicaid program. You and the Responsible Party agree to diligently take all steps necessary to apply for and obtain any available benefits. You and the Responsible Party further agree that this promise is separate from any promise to pay for care. This means that if, as a result of any failure or delay on your part or on the part of the Responsible Party to promptly apply for benefits and fully complete the application process when you are eligible for benefits, you and/or the Responsible Party will be liable for any loss suffered by us as a result of the failure or delay.

4.9. You and the Responsible Party shall comply and conform to all of our rules and policies currently in effect, as described in the "Patient and Resident Handbook" and as amended from time to time at our sole discretion. We will provide you with periodic notice during your stay, or as needed, of any change in the rules or policies. You shall also respect the personal rights and private property of other residents.

4.10 For the safety and peace of mind of all Facility residents, in addition to those prohibitions set forth in our current rules and policies, you shall not bring or keep any firearm, other dangerous instrument or illegal contraband in the Facility. You are prohibited from striking, assaulting, battering or threatening any person, including other residents, Facility staff or visitors. You agree that any violation of this Section renders you conclusively a danger to yourself and others, and subject to immediate discharge as provided in this Agreement. Any illegal activity shall also be reported to the appropriate authorities.

## Article V. Responsible Party

5.1. The Responsible Party represents and warrants that he or she has legal access to your income, assets and resources to pay for the services provided by us.

5.2. The Responsible Party shall execute the Responsible Party Agreement attached hereto at Exhibit C.

5.3. The Responsible Party does not, by reason of signing this Agreement, assume an obligation to reimburse us for your care, except from your income, assets and resources; however, the Responsible Party does assume other legal obligations as set forth in this Agreement and the Responsible Party Agreement and may be held legally responsible for failing to fulfill these obligations.

5.4. The Responsible Party shall provide us with his or her current home address and phone upon your admission and in the event of any change. If the Responsible Party fails to provide us with his or her current home address and phone, you and the Responsible Party waive any right the Responsible Party would otherwise have had to any notices.

5.5. If the Responsible Party executes this Agreement on the Resident's behalf, the Responsible Party represents that he or she is authorized to do so.

## Article VI. Payment and Financial Terms

6.1. You and/or the Responsible Party shall pay the daily private rate as set forth on Exhibit A. Daily charges will be billed in advance on a monthly basis. Payment for your first full month of care plus any days remaining in the month of admission shall be paid to us in advance upon admission. Bills are due and payable upon receipt. Bills not paid by the last day of the month are overdue.

6.2. As we are the primary provider of your healthcare services, room and board and other services as set forth at Exhibits A and B, You and/or the Responsible Party shall use your resources to satisfy any balance owed to us prior to expending Your resources for any other purpose.

6.3. A late fee of 1.5% of the outstanding balance shall be assessed on any unpaid balance due us as of the last day of each month, until paid in full.

6.4. Unless otherwise covered by Medicare, Medicaid, private insurance or other third-party payor, you and/or the Responsible Party shall pay for any item and/or service for which payment is not included in our daily rate as set forth on Exhibits "A" and "B" to this Agreement. Exhibits "A" and "B" to this Agreement set forth typical items and services for which we will charge separately, if any such item or service is requested by you. You are not required to request any such item or service.

6.5 Unless prohibited by Medicaid regulations, on the day of admission you and/or the Responsible Party shall pay a security deposit equal to one month's private pay payment (31 days) that we shall deposit in an interest bearing account to be held in escrow by us against which all of your unpaid financial obligations will be applied. You will be informed of the financial institution and the account number into which the payment was deposited within sixty (60) days of the establishment of the account. Interest earned, less any bank charges, will be credited to your account. Any balance remaining will be distributed to you or the Responsible Party within sixty (60) days after your transfer or discharge from the Facility, unless otherwise required by law.

6.6 In the event that your ability to pay the cost of care as herein provided is dependent upon the sale of any real estate owned by you, you hereby agree to execute a Note and Mortgage upon the real estate owned by you to secure any amounts owed to us presently or to become due in the future.

6.7 You and the Responsible Party acknowledge that you and/or Responsible Party are financially responsible to us for any charges not otherwise covered by Medicaid, Medicare or other third-party health care benefits. You and/or Responsible Party shall notify us of any changes in your health care coverage. In some cases, exact insurance benefits cannot be determined until the insurance company receives the claim.

6.8 You or the Responsible Party shall pay all costs, expenses and reasonable attorney fees in the event it becomes necessary for a legal guardian to be appointed for you, or an attorney's services are used by us to enforce any of the terms of this Agreement against you or the Responsible Party, including if suit is brought to collect any and all sums due and owing by you or the Responsible Party to us.

6.9 The Facility reserves the right to increase the per diem private pay rate and any and all other charges upon provision of a 30-day notice.

________(Your initials or the Responsible Party's initials)

## Article VII. Medicaid

7.1. You and the Responsible Party shall have the obligation to inform the Facility at least six (6) months prior to the time that the Resident's total assets and income will become less than the amounts specified by Medicaid for Medicaid eligibility or total assets of $2,000 or less, whichever is earlier, whereupon You and the Responsible Party shall submit an application to receive benefits under the Medicaid program.

7.2. You and the Responsible Party shall apply for and seek to establish eligibility and entitlement to receive benefits under the Medicare and/or Medicaid programs. You and the Responsible Party agree to diligently take all steps necessary to apply for and obtain any promise to pay for care. This means that if, as a result of any failure or delay on your part or on the part of the Responsible Party to promptly apply for benefits and fully complete the application process when you are eligible for benefits, you and/or the Responsible Party will be liable for any loss suffered by us as a result of the failure or delay, including but not limited to the private pay cost for any services not covered by the program.

7.3. You and the Responsible Party acknowledge that the submission of a timely and complete Medicaid application is the sole responsibility of the Resident/Responsible Party.

________(Your initials or the Responsible Party's initials)

7.4. You and the Responsible Party consent and authorize any and all persons or entities who have any information concerning your assets or income to disclose this information to us and to the County Welfare Agency and The County Board of Social Services or other Medicaid agency; You and the Responsible Party further authorize the County Welfare Agency and The County Board of Social Services or other Medicaid agency to release or disclose any information concerning, or relevant to, your Medicaid Application or eligibility to us.

7.5. In the event that you are determined to be entitled to benefits under the Medicaid program for some or all of the items and services provided by us to you:

(a) we shall accept the payments authorized and made by these programs, plus your contributions as required by these programs, as payment in full for only those items and services covered by these programs;

(b) you and the Responsible Party shall pay to us your income, "co-insurance" or "co-pay" amount as determined and required by the applicable program;

(c) if any of your security deposit had not been applied to your charges at the time you are determined to be eligible for Medicaid benefits, we will credit the unearned portion to your account;

(d) if you receive any monies from Medicare, Medicare Supplemental policy or any similar program in which you are enrolled, as payment or reimbursement for services rendered by us to you, you shall assign said monies to us.

7.6. Medicaid is a government program, and eligibility and payment decisions are ultimately made by government officials. Unless you are formally notified by Medicaid that all or any portion of our charges are to be paid by the Medicaid program, you are hereby informed that all of our charges shall be paid by you and/or the Responsible Party as set forth in this Agreement.

7.7. Medicaid Law requires that you pay to us all available income, as determined by Medicaid and indicated on the Form PR-1. This income will likely include your Social Security and Pension benefits. You and/or the Responsible Party, upon submission of an application for Medicaid benefits and in anticipation of finding that you are eligible for Medicaid benefits, shall submit to us, by the tenth (10th) day of each month, all of your income, including any benefit payments made by the Social Security Administration or any pension plan (less the Medicaid personal needs allowance or other allowances made by Medicaid, e.g. Medigap insurance premiums). Failure to pay us the amount of income determined by Medicaid shall constitute a violation of Medicaid Law.

________(Your initials or the Responsible Party's initials)

## Article VIII. Financial Disclosure

8.1. Notwithstanding any other provision of this Article, if, at the time of admission to the Facility, Medicaid has determined that you are eligible for Medicaid benefits to pay our charges, you are not required to comply with the financial disclosure requirements, except that you must provide or consent to have Medicaid provide documentation of your eligibility and of the amount and source(s) of your income Medicaid requires you to pay us.

8.2. You and the Responsible Party represent and warrant that, as part of completing our application for admission, you have disclosed all assets owned by you or in which you have any right (and the value of your share of ownership in each such asset), either solely or jointly with others, including all insurance policies; bank accounts; cash; real estate; investments; periodic income of any kind and character; automobiles; works of art; debts owed to you; security deposits owed to you; and liens held by you.

8.3. You and the Responsible Party represent and warrant that neither you nor anyone on your behalf have transferred, given, encumbered or changed the ownership of any of your assets, including any income, for less than full value, to any person, entity or to a trust of any form, during the past five (5) years.

________(Your initials or the Responsible Party's initials)

8.4. You and the Responsible Party agree, represent and warrant that neither you nor anyone on your behalf will perform, cause or allow the transfer, gift, encumbrance or change of ownership of any asset, including income, in such a manner as would cause you any period of Medicaid ineligibility.

________(Your initials or the Responsible Party's initials)

8.5. You and the Responsible Party agree, represent and warrant that any such transfer, gift, encumbrance or change in ownership as described in Section 8.4 shall be void. If you fail to bring a legal action to recover the asset disposed of under a void disposition, you hereby assign to us a right to bring a legal action against the person who received the asset to recover the full value of the asset, if possible; however, we are not required to do so.

8.6. You and the Responsible Party agree to provide us with an updated, accurate and complete set of Financial Disclosure Sheets, including disposition and location of assets, as reasonably requested, from time-to-time, by us.

## Article IX. Termination of Agreement / Discharge

9.1. You may transfer or discharge yourself from the Facility after providing at least three (3) days written notice to us before your transfer or discharge. If you leave, with or without notice, we shall have no further obligation to you, under the terms of this Agreement or otherwise, except as required by law. If you fail to give the required written notice prior to transfer or discharge, you will be obligated to pay a three day per diem charge, to be paid under the terms of this Agreement.

9.2. We may transfer or discharge you from the Facility for one or more of the following reasons upon thirty (30) days advance written notice to you and/or the Responsible Party:

(a) the transfer or discharge is necessary for your welfare and your needs cannot be met in the Facility;
(b) your medical condition no longer requires our care or services;
(c) the safety of individuals in the Facility is endangered;
(d) the health of individuals in the Facility would otherwise be endangered;
(e) you have not paid (or made arrangements to have paid) the fees you are obligated to pay for items and services you received;

(f) you have been determined to be mentally Ill, in accordance with Federal and State law, and we are unable to care for you;
(g) To comply with the clearly expressed and documented resident choice, or in conformance with the New Jersey Advance Directives for Health Care Act, as specified in N.J.A.C. 8:39-9.6(d);
(h) we cease to operate; or
(i) we cease to participate in the Medicare or Medicaid programs, for any reason, and your stay at the Facility is being paid for by Medicare or Medicaid.

9.3. We may transfer or discharge you for any reason noted above without thirty (30) days' notice in the event of an emergency or urgent medical need. In the event of transfer or discharge for such emergency reasons, notice shall be made as soon as practicable.

9.4. Upon your receipt of notice of discharge from the Facility for any reason, you and the Responsible Party shall participate in our discharge planning in order to arrange for an adequate, alternative placement for you, acceptable to the New Jersey Department of Health and Senior Services where required, including accepting your return to your home or the Responsible Party's home. If you will require any care after discharge, you and the Responsible Party agree to provide that care or to make arrangements, in conjunction with our discharge plan, to have that care provided to you. This promise is separate from any promise to pay for care. This means that if you or the Responsible Party fails to make suitable arrangements for your post-discharge location and/or care, you or the Responsible Party may be liable for any loss suffered by us as a result of that failure.

9.5 In the event that you are transferred for temporary hospitalization or therapeutic leave, and are a private pay resident, we will automatically hold your bed at the prevailing per diem rate unless you or your responsible party notify us that you do not want your bed held. If you are a Medicaid beneficiary, we will hold your bed for a period of ten (10) days as required by the Medicaid program.

If you are a Medicaid beneficiary and want to hold your bed after the ten day Medicaid bed hold period, you may do so by paying the prevailing private pay rate for your room. If you do not elect to hold your bed you will be deemed transferred and discharged by us.

9.6 Our policy is if you are deemed transferred and discharged under the provisions of Section 9.5, and you require the services provided by us, and you are eligible for Medicaid nursing facility services, you will be eligible to be readmitted to the next available and appropriate bed in a semi-private room in our facility. If you are readmitted under the provisions of this Section, you and the Responsible Party agree that all of the provisions of this Agreement shall resume in full force and effect, to the full extent permitted by law.

9.7 Payment in the aggregate amount of the daily charges for the first fourteen (14) days shall not be refunded in the event that you or the Responsible Party initiate a discharge prior to the expiration of the fourteenth day after admission. However, in the event of a discharge after fourteen (14) days, we shall refund any unused portion of any charges paid in advance to us, or your personal funds deposited with us, to you, your Legal Representative, executor or administrator, if one has been appointed, or any other person who has established to our satisfaction a legal right to the refund within sixty (60) days, unless we are instructed to do otherwise by the State Medicaid program.

9.8 Except as otherwise required by law, all of our obligations to you under this Agreement shall terminate upon your transfer or discharge from the Facility and all amounts owed to us under this Agreement shall be due immediately.

## Article X. Your Physician, Dentist, Pharmacy and Consent

10.1. You may choose a properly licensed personal physician from the list of physicians who have staff privileges at the facility.

The name of your physician is ______________________
The specialty of your physician is ______________________
The way of contacting your physician is (phone number) ______

10.2. You may choose a properly licensed dentist to be called in case of dental illness. In the event that you do not choose your own properly licensed dentist, we shall appoint a properly licensed dentist to provide services to you, as needed, at your expense.

The name of your dentist is______________________

If you choose a physician, dentist or other healthcare provider who does not have staff privileges at the Facility, you must travel, at your expense, to that healthcare provider to receive services from that provider. Physicians, dentists and other healthcare providers who do not have staff privileges at the Facility are prohibited from providing healthcare services at the Facility, except in cases of life-threatening emergency.

10.3.1 Pursuant to federal and state law, we shall control and monitor prescription medication instructions, labeling, storage and administration, and we record all medications released to you in your medical record. As a result, you agree that you will not bring any medications, whether prescription or over-the-counter, into the Facility, and you agree that you will obtain all of your prescription medications from the sub-contracted pharmacy which provides all prescription medications for the Facility.

10.4 You and the Responsible Party consent to the provision of routine nursing facility care by us to you in conjunction with your physician's orders and the plan of care developed by your care planning team, and acknowledge that you voluntarily have sought admission to us for such purpose.

________(Your Initials or the Responsible Party's Initials)

## Article XI. Healthcare Decision-Making/Power of Attorney.

11.1. You have the right to refuse medical treatment and to be informed of the consequences of refusing the treatment. Pursuant to a properly executed health care power of attorney, your health care power of attorney has the right under law to refuse medical treatment and to be informed of the consequences of refusing the treatment.

You **have / do not have** *(check one)* an advance directive for health care (living will/health care power of attorney), a true copy of which shall be attached to this Agreement and will be included in Resident's medical record.

________(Your Initials or the Responsible Party's Initials)

You **have / do not have** *(check one)* a completed Physician Order for Life-Sustaining Treatment (POLST), a true copy of which shall be attached to this Agreement and will be included in the Resident's medical record.

________(Your Initials or the Responsible Party's Initials)

11.2. While not required, we strongly suggest that you grant the Responsible Party or some other individual a power of attorney to act as attorney-in-fact presently or in the event that you become unable to manage your affairs.

My Power of Attorney has been granted to (copy attached).

## Article XII. Personal Possessions

12.1. Although we will take reasonable steps to protect your personal property, we have not expressly or implicitly assumed and do not assume any responsibility or liability for loss of or damage to any of your valuables, money, jewelry, eyeglasses, dentures, hearing aids, documents, furs, fur coats, or other personal property, except for money deposited with us under the delegation provisions of Sections 12.2 and 12.3 and except for small items you request and we accept for deposit in our safe. If we accept any item to be placed in our safe, we will give you a written receipt for it. We recommend that you personally insure any valuables in your possession at our facility.

12.2. You may manage your own financial affairs or, at any time, may delegate that responsibility to us by providing us with your written authorization.

12.3. You have determined that you wish us to manage your personal needs allowance.

________Yes________No

________(Your Initials or the Responsible Party's Initials)

## Article XIII. Release and Indemnification

13.1. We provide nursing facility care and services but are not an insurance company and are not an insurer of your safety or welfare and assume no liability as such.

13.2. We do not maintain a locked facility. You and the Responsible Party understand and agree that we cannot be held responsible if you leave the premises. We are also not responsible for your well-being or safety while under the care of any person not directly employed by us.

13.3. You and the Responsible Party agree to reimburse us for any damage, loss or injury caused, either directly or indirectly, by you.

13.4. You, the Responsible Party, and/or your personal representative, heirs and assigns, shall indemnify us and/or our employees, agents, volunteers and trustees for any and all claims, damages, liabilities and losses, including legal fees, associated with defending us and/or our employees, agents volunteers and/or trustees from any claim, whether civil or criminal in nature, arising from or in any manner connected with the performance of this Agreement and/or your stay at our facility; provided that, this obligation to indemnify shall not attach in any criminal action in which we and/or our employees, agents and volunteers either enters a plea of guilty or is adjudged guilty by a court of competent jurisdiction, all rights to appeal having been exhausted.

13.5. Notwithstanding the foregoing paragraphs, you and/or the Responsible Party have the right to obtain legal assistance and/or choose legal counsel, at your expense, or to file appropriate complaints, at your expense, subject to the provisions of this Article.

13.6. The provisions of this Article shall survive any termination of this Agreement.

## Article XIV. Arbitration

14.1. Any and all claims or controversies between you, the Responsible Party and us that arise out of your stay at the Facility, with the exception of eviction proceedings, and including but not limited to, violations of any right granted by law, including statutory resident's rights, or by this Admission Agreement, breach of contract, fraud or misrepresentation, negligence, gross negligence, malpractice or any other claim based on any alleged departure from accepted standards of medical or health care or safety, whether sounding in tort resulting in personal injury, or in contract, shall be submitted to binding arbitration, which shall be the sole means by which said claims or controversies shall be resolved.

**By agreeing to binding arbitration, each party hereby waives the right to a trial before a judge and/or a jury for all disputes including those at law or in equity but agrees to seek redress through binding arbitration.**

This arbitration requirement does not waive or limit any party's right to sue or otherwise assert any claims against the other party, but rather provides an alternative forum to exercise such right.

________(Your initials or the Responsible Party's initials)

14.2. Any demand for arbitration shall be made in writing by the demanding party and be submitted to the other party via certified mail, return receipt requested. The arbitration shall be conducted in the county in which the Facility is located.

14.3. The arbitration panel shall be composed of one (1) arbitrator. The parties shall agree upon an arbitrator who must either be a retired New Jersey Superior Court or federal judge or a member of the New Jersey Bar with at least ten 10 years of experience as an attorney. The arbitrator shall be independent of all parties, witnesses, and legal counsel, and no officer, director, affiliate, subsidiary, or employee of a party, witness, or legal counsel may serve as an arbitrator in the proceeding.

14.4. The arbitration hearing and other proceedings, including discovery, shall be conducted in accordance with the provisions of the New Jersey Arbitration Act of 2003 that do not conflict with the Federal Arbitration Act. Relief awarded, if any, shall be determined in accordance with the provisions of New Jersey law applicable to a comparable civil action. All matters relating to the arbitration, the arbitration proceedings and the arbitration award, shall remain confidential between the parties.

14.5. All fees of the arbitrator(s) shall be borne equally between the parties and each party agrees to bear its own attorneys' fees and costs.

14.6. This arbitration requirement shall bind us, our administrators, owners, officers, shareholders, representatives, directors, medical directors, employees, successors, assigns, agents, attorneys and insurers; and shall bind you and the Responsible Party, your successors, assigns, agents, attorneys, third party beneficiaries, insurers, heirs, trustees and representatives, including the personal representative or Executor of his/her estate.

All claims based in whole or in part on the same incident, transaction, or related course of care or services shall be arbitrated in one proceeding. Any claim of a party shall be waived and forever barred if it arose prior to the date upon which notice of arbitration is served and is not presented in the arbitration hearing.

**This binding arbitration provision of the admission agreement constitutes a binding legal agreement between the parties. You and/or the Responsible Party have read and understand this arbitration provision and understand that by signing this agreement you have waived your rights to a trial before a judge and/or a jury and voluntarily consent to all of the terms of this action. You and/or the Responsible party have been informed that you have the right to seek legal counsel concerning this section and agree to binding arbitration either upon consultation with an attorney or after affirmatively choosing not to seek advice of counsel.**

________(Your initials or the Responsible Party's initials)

## Article XV. Notices

15.1. All notices required by this Agreement shall be deemed to be given when personally delivered, sent by electronic mail or facsimile, sent by recognized overnight courier service, or placed into the custody of the United States Postal Service, addressed as follows:

(a) If to us: Administrator<br>**ABC NURSING HOME**<br>144 James Street<br>Townsville, State 54321

(b) If to you: (your name)<br>**ABC NURSING HOME**<br>James Street<br>Townsville, State 54321

15.2. Notice to the Responsible Party (in accordance with section 15.1) The Responsible Party agrees to provide us with his or her current home address and phone upon your admission and in the event of any change. If the Responsible Party fails to provide us with his or her current home address and phone, you and the Responsible Party waive any right you or the Responsible Party would otherwise have had to any notices.

## Article XVI. Resident's Rights

16.1. You acknowledge receipt of a copy of the Resident Bill of Rights.

________(Your initials or the Responsible Party's initials)

## Article XVII. Miscellaneous

17.1. You acknowledge receipt of a copy of the Disclosure and Consent Form which has been provided by the State Office of the Ombudsman for the Institutionalized Elderly.

________(Your initials or the Responsible Party's initials)

17.2. You acknowledge receipt of a copy of the Facility's notice of privacy practices for protected health information.

________(Your initials or the Responsible Party's initials)

17.3. You acknowledge receiving information concerning your legal right to make decisions about your medical care.

________(Your initials or the Responsible Party's initials)

17.4. You acknowledge receiving a copy of the Patient and Resident Handbook, which describes our current rules and regulations governing resident rights and responsibilities.

________(Your initials or the Responsible Party's initials)

17.5. You agree that while you are residing at the Facility, we may arrange to have your photograph taken which will become part of your medical record.

________(Your initials or the Responsible Party's initials)

17.6. You hereby grant us authorization to use your photograph for promotional or educational programs, provided that these pictures are used with dignity and discretion.

_______(Your initials or the Responsible Party's initials)

17.7. You authorize us to release your records, including any medical records, when you are transferred to another health care institution or when release of the records is required by law or by a third-party payer contract.

_______(Your initials or the Responsible Party's initials)

17.8. We expressly reserve the right to alter, change and amend any and all of the terms of this Agreement, including any and all charges upon thirty (30) days written notice to you and/or the Responsible Party. However, this Agreement may be changed on less than thirty (30) days' notice in order to comply with changes in State or Federal laws, regulations, policies or other requirements.

17.9. Our policy is to admit residents without regard to race, color, gender, sexual orientation, age, handicap or national origin.

17.10. In the event any provision of this Agreement is held to be invalid, illegal or unenforceable for any reason and in any respect, such invalidity, illegality or unenforceability shall in no event affect the remainder of this Agreement, which shall remain in full force and effect in accordance with its terms.

17.11. In the case of injury to you caused by a third-party, we are hereby granted the right of subrogation for all of our expenses incurred by reason of such injuries, although we are not required to pursue that right. This subrogation right shall not affect any other rights we may have to recover amounts owed us by you, including from the proceeds of any recovery by you from a third-party.

17.12. This Agreement is executed in and shall be construed in accordance with the laws of the State and shall be binding upon and inure to the benefit of us, you, the Responsible Party, if any, and the respective personal representatives, heirs, successors and assigns;

however, you may not assign any benefits or delegate any duties under this Agreement without the prior written, signed approval of us.

17.13. This Agreement represents the entire understanding and agreement of the parties and shall not be changed, amended, or terminated, except as specifically set forth in this Agreement.

The parties freely enter into this Agreement on the___day of___, 20_.

______________________________

______________________________

Your signature Responsible Party

______________________________

Our authorized signature

______________________________

(Name and Title)

# EXHIBIT "A"

PRIVATE PAY CHARGES

The daily rate for a private room is $

The daily rate for a semi-private room is $

The daily Private Pay rate includes:

- Room and board
- Nursing care
- Recreational and religious programming
- Dining services, including physician-ordered special diets
- Medical social services
- Laundry (linens and personal laundry)
- Housekeeping and maintenance

Items not included in the Private Pay daily rate for which you may be billed include:

- Hairdresser
- Personal telephone
- Transportation and escorts to appointments
- Cable television service
- Oxygen
- Incontinence and non-routine medical supplies
- Dietary supplements
- Prescription and over-the-counter medications
- Physician services*
- Rehabilitation Therapy (PT, OT, ST)*
- Laboratory charges*
- X-rays*

*Denotes items or services that are generally covered by Medicare Part B

# EXHIBIT "B"

MEDICAID CHARGES

The daily rate paid by the Medicaid program includes:

- Semi-private room
- Nursing Care
- Recreational and religious programming
- Dining services, including physician-ordered special diets
- Medical social services
- Laundry (linens and personal laundry)
- Housekeeping and maintenance
- Private room charge
- Oxygen
- Medical supplies
- Incontinence supplies
- Dietary supplements
- Over-the-counter medications
- Prescription medications authorized by Medicaid*
- Physician services*
- Rehabilitation Therapy (PT, OT, ST)*
- Laboratory charges*
- X-rays*

*Denotes items or services that are generally covered by Medicare Part B and Medicaid Items not covered in the Medicaid daily rate and for which you may be billed include:

- Hairdresser
- Personal telephone
- Transportation and escorts to appointments
- Cable television service

# EXHIBIT "C"

## RESPONSIBLE PARTY AGREEMENT

This Responsible Party Agreement (the "Agreement") is made between **ABC Nursing Home** (the "Facility") and_, the legal representative or representative individual (the "Responsible Party") of______________, (the "Resident").

WHEREAS, the Responsible Party and Facility enter into this Agreement to facilitate the provision of care to the Resident.

WHEREAS, the Responsible Party may be the Guardian, the Agent under a valid Power of Attorney, or any person authorized by Resident to serve as Resident's Responsible Party.

WHEREAS, Facility shall discuss and consult with Responsible Party regarding pertinent decisions related to Resident's stay and care at the Facility.

THEREFORE, Facility and Responsible Party agree to the following terms and conditions:

1. Responsible Party affirms that the information provided in the Admission Agreement and related documents are true and correct to the best of his or her knowledge. Responsible Party acknowledges that the submission of any false information, misrepresentation or lack of disclosure may result in the termination of the Admission Agreement and may result in the discharge of the Resident from the Facility at the Resident and/or Responsible Party's expense.
2. Responsible Party affirms that he or she has access to Resident's income and resources and that Resident's income and resources are available to pay for Resident's care in the Facility. The Responsible Party shall pay Facility from Resident's financial resources for services and supplies provided to Resident in accordance with the Admission Agreement.
3. When the Resident's financial resources warrant it, Responsible Party shall take any and all actions necessary and appropriate to initiate, make and conclude application for Medical Assistance

("Medicaid") benefits on behalf of the Resident, including providing all necessary documentation, complying with deadlines and pursuing all necessary appeals. Responsible Party shall exercise diligent efforts in the application and appeal processes to assure benefits from any third party or government payor. Responsible Party shall utilize Resident's income and resources only for Resident and shall not utilize any of Resident's income or resources for Responsible Party's benefit nor transfer any of Resident's real property except for proceeds at fair market value for the benefit of Resident.

In the event Resident applies for Medicaid, Responsible Party shall pay the applicable Resident Income to Facility on a monthly basis. The Resident Income is determined by the local Medicaid office or County Board of Social Services ("CBOSS") and set forth on Form PR-1. Responsible Party, at the request of Facility and to the extent permitted by law, shall immediately sign over and/or designate the Facility as the representative/designated payee for any income available to Resident in an amount not to exceed the Resident Income. Responsible Party should take whatever action as may be necessary to insure that such payments are made directly to Facility.

4. Responsible Party understands that if he or she fulfills his or her obligation under this Agreement, he or she shall not be held personally liable for the Resident's charges. This Agreement shall not be construed or operate as a third party guaranty.
5. Responsible Party acknowledges that he or she has received a copy of the Admission Agreement and understands the terms and conditions contained therein.
6. Responsible Party acknowledges that he or she has reviewed this Responsible Party Agreement and understands the information set forth herein.

IN WITNESS WHEREOF, the parties, intending to be legally bound hereby, have signed this Responsible Party Agreement on this day of_____, 20_____.

# APPENDIX 4

## Fact Sheet on Nursing-Home Agreements

**REPRINTED WITH PERMISSION FROM CALIFORNIA ADVOCATES FOR NURSING HOME REFORM**

## Nursing Home Admission Agreements

When you are admitted to a nursing home, you will be asked to sign an admission agreement that explains your rights and responsibilities and those of the nursing home. In years past, this involved signing contracts written by nursing homes that often contained deceptive or illegal terms.

California is the first state in the nation to outlaw the use of admission contracts written by nursing homes. By law (SB 1061, 1997), all California nursing homes must now use the Standard Admission Agreement developed by the California Department of Public Health. (California Health and Safety Code §1599.61) After more than a decade of delays, the Standard Admission Agreement took effect on April 6, 2012.

The Standard Admission Agreement's purpose is to give you peace of mind that you are signing a document that protects your rights and does not expose you or your family to unexpected financial liability. It is important, however, for you to read the document carefully and to make sure you fully understand its terms before you sign it.

### The Agreement

The California Department of Public Health has posted the Standard Admission Agreement (CDPH 327) and its attachments on its website. The Standard Admission Agreement is available in English, Chinese, Korean, Spanish, Vietnamese and Braille.

The Standard Admission Agreement consists of the basic Agreement and the following attachments:

- Attachment A—Facility Owner and Licensee Identification
- Attachment B-1—Supplies and Services Included in the Basic Daily Rate for Private Pay and Privately Insured Residents
- Attachment B-2—Optional Supplies and Services Not Included in the Basic Daily Rate for Private Pay and Privately Insured Residents

- Attachment C-1—Supplies and Services Included in the Basic Daily Rate for Medi-Cal Residents
- Attachment C-2—Supplies and Services Not Included in the Medi-Cal Basic Daily Rate That Medi-Cal Will Pay the Dispensing Provider for Separately
- Attachment C-3—Optional Supplies and Services Not Covered by Medi-Cal That May Be Purchased by Medi-Cal Residents
- Attachment 0-1—Supplies and Services Covered by the Medicare Program for Medicare Residents
- Attachment 0-2—Optional Supplies and Services Not Covered by Medicare That May Be Purchased by Medicare Residents
- Attachment E—Authorization for Disclosure of Medical Information
- Attachment F—Resident Bill of Rights

## Before Signing the Agreement

Before signing the Standard Admission Agreement:

Read it and its attachments carefully;

- List any questions about your rights and responsibilities;
- Make sure that all your questions are answered to your satisfaction before signing;

Use the Agreement as an opportunity to clarify expectations and to negotiate care needs and costs.

- Consult an attorney or advocate if you have concerns or questions about the Agreement.

Carefully review the actual written Agreement the nursing home is asking you to sign. Do not rely on the standard version of the Agreement on the Department of Public Health website. Although a nursing home cannot legally alter or amend the Agreement unless it receives written permission from the California Department of Health Public Health (Title 22 California

Code of Regulations §73518), it is possible that a nursing home may have altered the Agreement with or without the required permission.

Please inform CANHR if a nursing home asks you to sign an Agreement that has been significantly altered from its standard terms.

## Signing the Agreement

The person being admitted to the nursing home is the only person required to sign the Standard Admission Agreement. (California Health & Safety Code §1599.65) Section I (Preamble) of the Agreement states:

If you are able to do so, you are required to sign this Agreement in order to be admitted to this Facility. If you are not able to sign this Agreement, your representative may sign it for you.

Make sure you obtain a copy of the signed Agreement and any other documents presented or signed at admission. Section XII of the Agreement requires the facility to give you a copy of the signed agreement, all attachments, any other documents you sign at admission, and a receipt for any payments you make at admission, upon your request.

## Financial Responsibility of Residents' Representatives Who Sign the Agreement

The resident is responsible for paying any nursing home bills under the Agreement, not his or her family or friends. (Title 42 United States Code §1396r(c)(5), Title 42 Code of Federal Regulations §483.12(d)(2), California Welfare & Institutions Code §14110.8)

Signing the Standard Admission Agreement as a resident's representative does not make you responsible for using your own money to pay for care provided by the nursing home. Section II (Identification of Parties to this Agreement) of the Agreement states:

**IF OUR FACILITY PARTICIPATES IN THE MEDI-CAL OR MEDICARE PROGRAM, OUR FACILITY DOES NOT REQUIRE THAT YOU HAVE ANYONE**

**GURANTEE PAYMENT FOR YOUR CARE BY SIGNING OR COSIGNING THIS ADMISSION AGREEMENT AS A CONDITION OF ADMISSION.**

Additionally, it states:

Signing this Agreement as a Resident's Representative does not, in and of itself, make the Resident's Representative liable for the Resident's debts. However, a Resident's Representative acting as the Resident's financial conservator or otherwise responsible for distribution of the Resident's monies shall provide reimbursements from the Resident's assets to the Facility in compliance with Section V. of the agreement.

The resident's authorized financial representative is responsible to use the resident's funds to pay nursing home fees, such as a share-of-cost set by Medi-Cal for a resident on Medi-Cal. (California Welfare & Institutions Code §14110.8)

## Signing Other Documents at Admission

You and your representative cannot be required to sign any other document at the time of admission or as a condition of admission or continued stay in a California nursing home. (Title 22 California Code of Regulations §73518) This right is stated in Section I, the Preamble to the Agreement.

Do not sign any forms or documents that conflict with the Standard Admission Agreement or attempt to restrict your rights. Avoid signing any documents that seek waiver of liability, binding arbitration or general consent to treatment. The Agreement already includes a general consent to treatment and emergency care in Section III so additional forms are not needed for this purpose at admission.

Although you are not required to sign other documents, the nursing home may ask you to do so. It is usually best not to sign other documents at admission. Ask the nursing home to give you copies of any forms to review in advance before making decisions about signing them.

If you have any concerns or doubts about a document you are asked to sign, seek advice from a qualified attorney or advocate before doing so.

## Binding Arbitration Agreement

Do not sign a binding arbitration agreement at admission. Nursing homes use arbitration agreements to prevent residents from being able to sue for abuse or neglect.

By signing a binding arbitration agreement, you give up your constitutional right to go to court if a dispute arises in the facility, even if it involves abuse or neglect. There is no right to appeal a decision made through binding arbitration.

Nursing homes cannot require you to sign an arbitration agreement and cannot present an arbitration agreement as part of the Standard Admission Agreement. (California Health & Safety Code §1599.81, Title 22 California Code of Regulations §73518). Any arbitration agreement shall be separate from the Standard Admission Agreement and shall contain the following advisory in large, bold type at the top of the agreement:

**Residents shall not be required to sign this arbitration agreement as a condition of admission to this facility, and cannot waive the ability to sue for violation of the Resident Bill of Rights.**

Residents and their legal representatives can rescind an arbitration agreement by giving written notice to the facility within 30 days of their signature. (California Code of Civil Procedure §1295)

To learn more about problems with binding arbitration, read **CANHR's fact sheet** on this subject.

## Advance Directives

At admission, the nursing home should ask you for a copy of your advance directive and, if you don't have one, may suggest you establish one. Although it is a good idea to have an advance directive, nursing homes cannot require you to have or to make one as a condition of admission or continued stay. This issue is addressed in Section III, Consent to Treatment, in the Standard Admission Agreement.

Advance directive is the general term used to describe instructions you give someone about preferences for your future medical treatment. At admission, the nursing home must give you written information about advance directives explaining: (1) your right to direct your own health care decisions; (2) your right to accept or refuse medical treatment; (3) your right under California law to prepare an advance health care directive; and (4) the facility's policies that govern the use of advance directives. (Title 42 United States Code §§1395cc(f), 1396r(c)(2)(E) & 1396a(w), Title 42 Code of Federal Regulations §§489.1 02, 483.1 O(b )(8) & 431.20)

There are different types of advance directives. The following types are examples, not a complete list.

An Advance Health Care Directive (AHCD), also known as a Power of Attorney for Health Care, allows you to appoint an agent to make health care decisions for you. Your agent only makes decisions for you if you have lost capacity, unless you state otherwise in the document. You can give an agent limited or broad powers in an AHCD, from the right to access medical records to the power to make anatomical gifts. You may also specify healthcare instructions you want to be followed. All adults should have an AHCD.

A Physician Order for Life-Sustaining Treatment (POLST) is another form of advance health care planning where your or your legally authorized surrogate can express end-of-life preferences. The form instructs providers about what to do regarding CPR, comport care measure, artificial nutrition and hydration, and other important treatments. A POLST must be signed by a physician and is thus an actual medical order that nurses and nursing assistants must follow. The document is meant for people who are terminally ill as a way to control their end-of-life care.

In recent years, some nursing homes have told residents and their representatives that a POLST form is required at admission. This is not true. Establishing a POLST is a choice, not a requirement. To learn about the pros and cons of POLST, read **CANHR's report** on this subject. To learn more about advance directives, read **CANHR's fact sheet**.

## Participation in Medi-Cal and Medicare

The admission agreement must clearly state whether the nursing home participates in the MediCal and Medicare programs. (California Health & Safety

Code §§1599.66 & 1439.8, California Welfare & Institutions Code §14022.3) This information is found in Section V (Financial Arrangements) of the Standard Admission Agreement.

If a nursing home is withdrawing from the Medi-Cal program, it must include this information in Section V (Financial Arrangements) of the Agreement and give the date that it notified the Department of Health Care Services of its intent to withdraw from Medi-Cal. A nursing home that is withdrawing from Medi-Cal is not required to accept Medi-Cal for residents admitted after it notified the State of its intent to withdraw. The Standard Admission Agreement explains that residents admitted on or before the date of the withdrawal notice can use Medi-Cal to pay for their care, even if they become eligible for Medi-Cal after that date. (California Welfare & Institutions Code §14022.4, Title 42 United States Code §1396r(c)(2)(F))

## Requirements to Pay Privately

It is illegal for a Medicare or Medi-Cal certified nursing home to require a resident to pay privately for any set period of time. (Title 42 United States Code §§1395i-3(c)(5)(A) & 1396r(c)(5)(A), and Title 42 Code of Federal Regulations §483.12(d)) When a resident qualifies for Medi-Cal or Medicare nursing home coverage, nursing homes certified by these programs must accept their payments. (California Health & Safety Code § 1599.69 & 1599.76, California Welfare & Institutions Code §14019.3, and Title 42 Code of Federal Regulations §483.1 0(b)(10))

Section V of the Agreement on Financial Arrangements includes the following statement:

**You should be aware that no facility that participates in the Medi-Cal program may require any resident to remain in private pay status for any period of time before converting to Medi-Cal coverage. Nor, as a condition of admission or continued stay in such a facility, may the facility require oral or written assurance from a resident that he or she is not eligible for, or will not apply for, Medicare or Medi-Cal benefits.**

Some nursing homes require applicants to disclose financial information that is used to project how long they can pay privately before qualifying for Medi-Cal. Applicants with more money are usually given preference. Although this practice is of questionable legality, federal and California authorities are doing nothing to stop it.

## Notice About Medi-Cal Eligibility

Prior to admission, Medi-Cal certified nursing homes must notify you about Medi-Cal eligibility standards, using a **State mandated notice**. (California Welfare & Institutions Code §§14006.3 & 14006.4) The legislature required the notice after learning that some nursing homes misinformed applicants and residents about Medi-Cal eligibility.

The notice contains important information, including:

- You do not have to use all your resources to qualify;
- Your home is an exempt resource. Its value does not affect your eligibility, and you have the right to transfer the home;
- Medi-Cal has special rules for married couples that protect resources and income for the spouse who is not in the nursing home.

## Deposits

A nursing home cannot require or accept a deposit if Medi-Cal or Medicare is helping to pay for your stay. (California Health & Safety Code § 1599. 70, California Welfare & Institutions Code §14110.9, Title 42 Code of Federal Regulations §489.22 & 483.12(d)(3))

Nursing homes may require a deposit if you are paying privately for your care. Deposits paid by private paying residents must be returned when Medi-Cal or Medicare start paying for their nursing home care. (California Welfare & Institutions Code §1411 0.8 & Health & Safety Code §1599.70)

This issue is addressed in Section V(B) of the Agreement on Security Deposits.

## Rate Changes

If a nursing home plans to increase its daily rate or service fees, it must give residents 30 days written notice of the changes. (California Health & Safety Code §1288, 1599.67)

## Refunds and Charges Following Discharges

You cannot be charged for any days of care after discharge or death and are entitled to a refund of any advance payments made to the nursing home. (California Health & Safety Code § 1599.71) See Section V of the Agreement on Financial Arrangements. The only exception is if you leave the nursing home voluntarily within three days of admission, in which case you may be charged for up to three days at the basic daily rate if Medicare or Medi-Cal are not paying for your nursing home care.

If you are due a refund after your discharge, the nursing home must pay it to you within 14 days of your leaving the facility. See Section V(E) of the Agreement on Payment of Other Refunds to You.

If a resident dies, any advance payments must be returned to the heir, legatee or personal representative of the resident within two weeks after discharge or death. (California Health & Safety Code §1599.71 (a) and Title 22 California Code of Regulations §72531)

## Discharge Notice

The Admission Agreement shall not require a resident to provide advance notice of when he or she is moving out of a facility. (California Health & Safety Code §1599.71.)

## Personal Possessions

At admission, the nursing home must establish a personal property inventory and give you or your representative a copy. (California Health & Safety Code §1289.4) Keep the inventory sheet current and save a copy.

The nursing home is also required to give you a copy of its policies and procedures regarding protection of your personal property and the state laws that require those policies. (California Health & Safety Code §§1289.3, 1289.4,1289.5 & 1418.7) See Section VIII of the Agreement on Personal Property and Funds.

## Confidentiality

You have a right to confidential treatment of your medical and health information. (California Health & Safety Code §1599.73, Title 22 California Code of Regulations §72527(a)(1 0) &72543(b), Title 42 United States Code §§1395i-3(c)(1 )(A)(iv) & 1396r(c)(1 )(A)(iv), and Title 42 Code of Federal Regulations §483.1 O(e)). You may authorize the nursing home to disclose medical information about you to a family member or other person by completing Attachment E to the Standard Admission

## Your rights

The Standard Admission Agreement is intended to inform you about your rights as a nursing home resident. Certain rights are discussed within the Agreement, but Attachment F (Bill of Rights) is a more comprehensive description of your rights. It is a verbatim collection of selected federal and state laws and regulations. Attachment F, however, is 39 pages long and not an easy way to learn about your rights.

**CANHR's fact sheet** on this subject provides a quicker way to learn about your rights.

Admission Agreement Complaints

If your Agreement, the "Authorization for Disclosure of Medical Information" form nursing home is not using the Standard Admission Agreement or violates any of your rights, you may file a formal complaint with the California Department of Public Health. For information on filing a complaint, see CANHR's fact sheet, **How to File a Nursing Home Complaint** . You can also contact your attorney, local ombudsman program or CANHR to discuss your concerns. **BE SURE TO REQUEST AND KEEP A SIGNED COPY OF THE ADMISSION AGREEMENT!**

http://www.canhr.org/factsheets/nhjs/html/fs_.admissionagreement.htm